New Perspectives

FENG SHUI

MAN-HO KWOK is a leading Feng Shui master throughout Europe. He studied for twenty years before qualifying, and is now in considerable demand as a consultant on Feng Shui. He is the internationally acclaimed author and translator of numerous books on Chinese wisdom, including *The Tao Te Ching* and *The Illustrated Tao Te Ching*, both published by Element.

JOANNE O'BRIEN is a well-known authority on Chinese religion and philosophy, and is the author of a number of popular books on Chinese matters including *The Contemporary I Ching*, *Chinese Myths and Legends* and *Lines of Destiny* (Chinese face and hand divination).

The Series

New Perspectives provide attractive and accessible introductions to a comprehensive range of mind, body and spirit topics. Beautifully designed and illustrated, these practical books are written by experts in each subject.

Titles in the series include:

ALEXANDER TECHNIQUE
by Richard Brennan

AROMATHERAPY
by Christine Wildwood

DREAMS
by David Fontana

FENG SHUI
by Man-Ho Kwok with Joanne O'Brien

FLOWER REMEDIES
by Christine Wildwood

HOMEOPATHY
by Peter Adams

MASSAGE
by Stewart Mitchell

MEDITATION
by David Fontana

NLP
by Carol Harris

NUMEROLOGY
by Rodford Barrat

REFLEXOLOGY
by Inge Dougans

TAROT
by A T Mann

New Perspectives

FENG SHUI

An Introductory Guide to the Chinese Way to Harmony

MAN-HO KWOK WITH JOANNE O'BRIEN

ELEMENT

Shaftesbury, Dorset • Boston, Massachusetts
Melbourne, Victoria

First published as *The Elements of Feng Shui* in 1991
by Element Books Limited

This revised edition first published in Great Britain in 1999 by
Element Books Limited, Shaftesbury, Dorset SP7 8BP

Published in the USA in 1999 by
Element Books, Inc.,
160 North Washington Street,
Boston, MA 02114

Published in Australia in 1999 by
Element Books and distributed by
Penguin Australia Limited
487 Maroondah Highway,
Ringwood, Victoria 3134

Designed for Element Books Limited by
Design Revolution, Queens Park Villa,
30 West Drive, Brighton, East Sussex BN2 2GE

ELEMENT BOOKS LIMITED
Editorial Director: Sarah Sutton
Editorial Manager: Jane Pizzey
Commissioning Editor: Grace Cheetham
Production Director: Roger Lane

DESIGN REVOLUTION
Editorial Director: Ian Whitelaw
Art Director: Lindsey Johns
Editor: Julie Whitaker
Designer: Vanessa Good

Printed and bound in Great Britain by
Bemrose Security Printing, Derby

British Library Cataloguing in Publication data available

Library of Congress Cataloging in Publication data available

ISBN 1-86204-628-X

Contents

ACKNOWLEDGEMENTS

With thanks to Elizabeth Breuilly, Kerry Brown, Jo Edwards and Martin Palmer for their help and support.

INTRODUCTION

Why do some places emit a sense of well-being and peace and other places a feeling of unease? How is it that some businesses seem dogged by bad luck and others are blessed by success?

To a feng shui master the answer is easy – the forces at work in the cosmos and the land are in chaos in one place and in harmony in another. If the site and orientation of a particular building clashes with the contours of the land, the flow of a river or the direction of a road, if the position of a front door or a piece of furniture blocks the flow of ch'i, the life-giving energy, then misfortune will usually follow as a matter of course.

What Is Feng Shui?

Feng shui is the ancient Chinese science of creating harmony. It is not a matter of luck and is much more than a system of omens. In the West, breaking a mirror is considered a bad omen, and there is little that can be done about it once the deed is done. In the East, however,

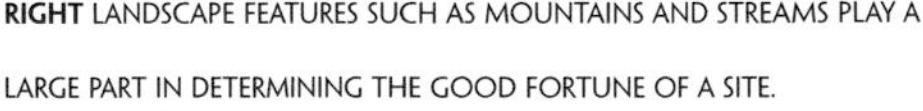

RIGHT LANDSCAPE FEATURES SUCH AS MOUNTAINS AND STREAMS PLAY A LARGE PART IN DETERMINING THE GOOD FORTUNE OF A SITE.

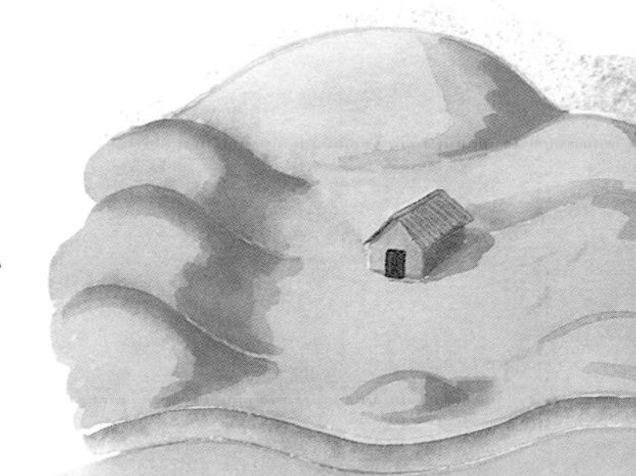

CH'I

Ch'i is the invisible energy that surrounds us at all times. Ch'i has no shape and no form, but exists in all things, both animate and inanimate. Ch'i can be auspicious (known as sheng ch'i, the dragon's cosmic breath) or inauspicious (known as shar ch'i, the dragon's killing breath), and feng shui practice aims to nourish beneficial ch'i.

YIN/YANG

The ancient Chinese symbol of yin/yang represents the two universal forces that underpin the structure of both Heaven and Earth. Yin and yang are opposites, yet they complement one another – one cannot exist without the other. When there is balance between yin and yang, there is harmony.

Yin is female, dark, night, cold, passive. Yang is male, light, day, hot, energy.

ABOVE THE YIN YANG SYMBOL REPRESENTS THE COMPLEMENTARY OPPOSITES THAT ARE THE BASIC TENETS OF CHINESE PHILOSOPHY. ALTHOUGH OPPOSITES, WHEN COMBINED, THEY REFLECT PERFECT HARMONY.

it is considered bad luck to have a tree planted directly outside the front door. Fortunately, in this case something can be done to counteract any ill-effects. By following the basic principles of feng shui, individuals can actively shape fate instead of merely being its passive recipients.

Feng shui literally means 'wind and water'. These are the elemental forces that shape the landscape and that have the hidden powers to affect human fortune. These forces are at work everywhere, in many forms, particularly in the flow of ch'i and in the balance of yin and yang (*see* box p.8). Ch'i is continually on the move, condensing, evaporating, inhaling and exhaling. If the flow of ch'i is blocked by a door of a building, it may cause disaster. By contrast, ch'i can also evaporate in a space that is too open. Yin and yang are opposing forces in a continual state of flux and tension. They represent female and male, light and dark, water and fire; they are in everything that exists. The feng shui expert is familiar with the flow of ch'i and the balance of yin and yang across the landscape and through buildings or cemeteries. Armed with this knowledge, he is able to advise on the design and planning of new buildings as well as identifying the source of any bad luck in an existing building.

Knowledge of feng shui is not, however, the prerogative of the feng shui master. Although an expert has a highly detailed knowledge of the mysterious workings of the universe through the study of Chinese arts and sciences, there are many simple and practical principles that anyone can follow. Many involve common sense, others are learned and others involve intuition (*see* chapters 5–8). For example, a house that is built on low-lying ground is likely to flood during heavy rains. Similarly, a tree planted too close to the house is likely to affect the foundations. This is bad feng shui.

At other times the view from a building may be pleasing to the eye and provide the inhabitants with a sense of well-being. That in itself is positive feng shui.

Feng shui is often referred to as geomancy, more commonly known in the West as 'earth magic'. Feng shui does, however, embrace more

Good Fortune Charms

Many Chinese people hang a ba-gua, a small mirror surrounded by lines known as trigrams, outside restaurants, homes or offices. This mirror will deflect any bad fortune that may by caused by the position of the front door or the direction of the road facing the building. Sometimes the mirror alone is not powerful enough to deflect bad fortune, and wind chimes are also hung in the doorway to ward off ghosts and spirits who fear their sound. If the mirror or chimes are not sufficient to resolve bad feng shui, then structural alterations may be necessary and many family businesses are willing to carry the cost of expensive alterations.

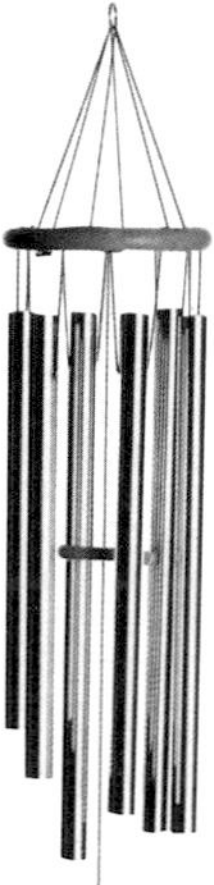

LEFT WIND CHIMES ARE OFTEN HUNG ABOVE A DOOR TO DEFLECT HARMFUL CH'I.

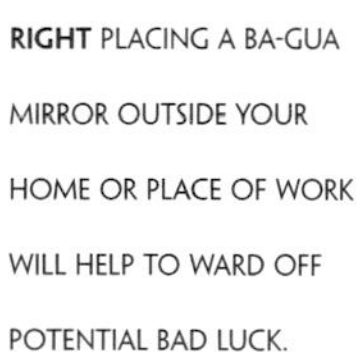

RIGHT PLACING A BA-GUA MIRROR OUTSIDE YOUR HOME OR PLACE OF WORK WILL HELP TO WARD OFF POTENTIAL BAD LUCK.

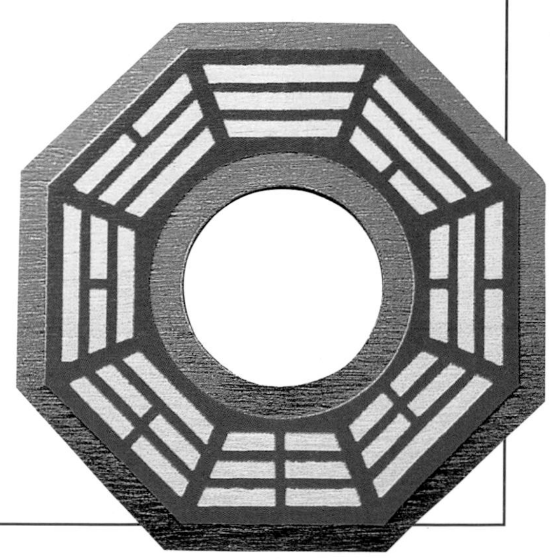

than Western geomancy. Not only is it part of everyday life, catering for the physical comforts, mental well-being and financial security of the individual, but it also harnesses far greater cosmic forces, which are believed to affect the universe. Through the use of the Lo Pan compass, the feng shui expert works to align human activity with these forces (*see* Tools of the Geomancer, p.93).

Feng shui is now becoming increasingly popular in the West. It can be seen as a development of traditional Western geomantic practices, adding a more sympathetic dimension to the relationship between people, structures and their environment. While most people outside the Chinese community would find it strange to pay for the services of a feng shui expert before buying a house, it is not unusual for businesses in the United Kingdom and elsewhere to pay for such a survey. However, once you are familiar with the basic rules of practical feng shui, there may be no need to call in an expert. An expert would say that if you believe in the power of feng shui and know where to look, you can reverse your misfortune as well as improving your mental and physical well-being. For many, the power of feng shui is a matter of life and death and they believe that careful planning can avert tragedy.

The outward signs of feng shui are most obvious in Hong Kong and other Chinese communities throughout the world. Before a new building is constructed in Hong Kong the designers will consult a feng shui expert. When the Hong Kong and Shanghai Bank was built it was the tallest building in the area, a sign of authority. The building faced north, a favourable direction for this site, it had the protection of the hill known as the 'Peak' behind and the good fortune to be on a slight gradient that led down to the wide, open space of Hong Kong harbour. Meanwhile, the Bank of China, who were building a new bank nearby, delayed their construction until work on the Hong Kong and Shanghai Bank was completed. In order to gain financial superiority in the monetary dealings of Hong Kong, the Bank of China built their bank slightly higher than the Hong Kong and Shanghai Bank. The construction of the bank also adversely affected the feng

ABOVE MUCH OF HONG KONG'S PROSPERITY CAN BE ATTRIBUTED TO ITS EXTREMELY AUSPICIOUS SITING. MOREOVER, MOST OF ITS BUILDINGS ARE DESIGNED WITH GOOD FENG SHUI PRACTICE IN MIND.

shui of other nearby businesses – the reflective windows of the Bank of China turned bad fortune back on to its neighbours and the sharp corners of the building acted like daggers, slicing through neighbouring businesses. To avert further bad luck, and to protect clients and staff, the managing directors of neighbouring office blocks hung ba-gua mirrors or small tridents on the outside walls of their offices to stave off the ill-effects of the sharp corners. A third office block, known as Central Plaza, has been built on Hong Kong Island – it is the tallest building in the area, and has symbolic financial dominance over all the surrounding businesses.

When I lived in Hong Kong, I knew of a married couple who had lived happily for more than 50 years in their farmhouse in the New Territories. They had raised three sons and two daughters. Their daughters had married and gone to live with their in-laws; two sons had also married and brought their wives to live in the farmhouse. Between them the sons had three grandchildren, and when a third son was due to marry the parents realized they could not offer the new couple a bedroom of their own in the family home.

Determined to keep the family under one roof, they arranged for an extension to be built to the right-hand side of the house. The extension was completed within a month and immediately after their marriage the youngest son and his new wife moved into the house. Three months after their marriage the youngest son was electrocuted while trying to fix an old electric fan. Three months later, the second son died in a road accident, and a fortnight later his mother died of a serious illness. The father could not believe that he should lose three members of his family in the space of a year. Grief-stricken, he turned to his friends and neighbours for advice. Although the feng shui of the house had been assessed before it was built, the neighbours suggested a feng shui master should visit once again to identify the source of this misfortune.

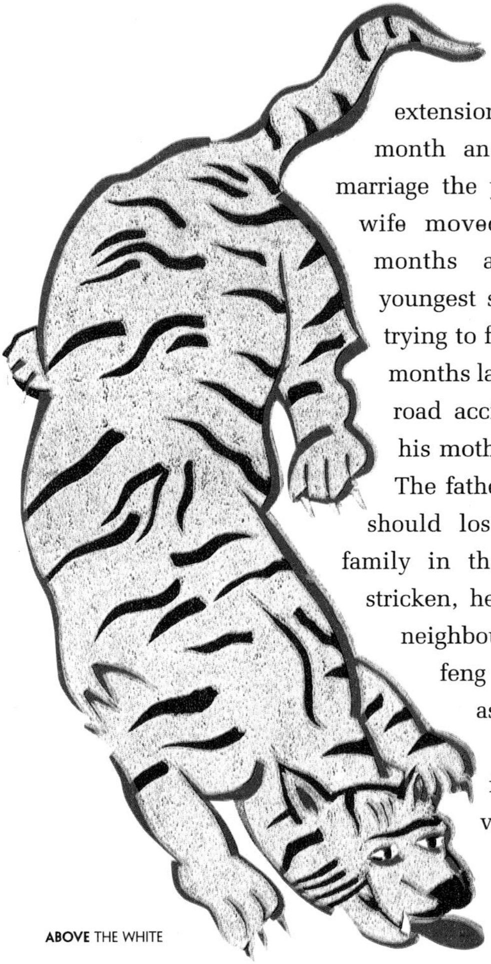

ABOVE THE WHITE TIGER WILL PROTECT YOUR HOME. HOWEVER, IF ITS SPIRIT BECOMES TOO STRONG, THE TIGER WILL OVERCOME THE GREEN DRAGON, CAUSING BAD FENG SHUI.

When the feng shui master arrived he drew out his compass and carefully checked the main door, and every room in the house. The positioning of the rooms and furniture was perfect and the master was puzzled. He checked the back of the house where the pigs and poultry were kept and once again the reading appeared to be excellent. Even the hill behind the house protected the family from both bad weather and misfortune. When he moved to front of the house and came across the extension, however, he knew why the family had suffered such tragedy.

'Knock this extension down immediately', he ordered. 'This is the source of your unhappiness. The spirit of the White Tiger resides on the right-hand side of your house and the spirit of the Green Dragon on the left. Since you have built the extension, the Tiger has become so powerful that the Green Dragon can no longer control it. The Tiger is now free to roam your house and to consume those who live there.'

The family might have had better luck had they consulted the Chinese Almanac before choosing a day to start the construction, or they could have hung powerful charms to offset the bad feng shui. The situation would even have been better if they had built the extension on the left-hand side of the house, the side of the Green Dragon.

ABOVE THE GREEN DRAGON IS ONE OF THE FOUR CELESTIAL ANIMALS. ITS POWER SHOULD BE BALANCED WITH THAT OF THE WHITE TIGER FOR GOOD FENG SHUI.

The feng shui master pointed out to the family that this structural imbalance would always bring misfortune, and he could only suggest that they demolish the extension.

LEFT A FENG SHUI RULER, COMPASS AND PA KUA ARE USED TO DETERMINE THE FENG SHUI OF A PARTICULAR ROOM OR LOCATION.

Not all structural mistakes have such severe consequences as the example above, and most can be resolved without resorting to demolition or extensive rebuilding. According to feng shui principles, fortunes can be improved by rearranging furniture, changing the internal decor or by making small structural alterations in the home or office.

On a recent visit to Hong Kong, I was invited to lunch by a friend who ran a clothing factory. During the course of the meal, the man admitted that his business was in trouble, and that if trade continued to decline he would be bankrupt within the year. He knew his factory was well-sited and for years his business had been flourishing. However, since moving to a new apartment his luck had changed.

I agreed to visit his friend's house and, after choosing an auspicious day for a feng shui reading from the Chinese Almanac, he arranged the visit. As soon as I entered the living room I spotted the source of my friend's financial problems. A door had been built linking the living room to the dining room at a position in the room known as the wealthy point. The good fortune that should have accumulated at this point was disappearing through the doorway and into the dining room. The ch'i, or life-giving energy, was dispersing in too many directions.

I then used my compass to assess all the other rooms in the house – the feng shui proved to be perfect. The following day the door was filled in and a new one was built further down the wall. Three months later I was invited to a celebratory dinner by my friend who informed me that business had never been better.

RIGHT THE CHINESE ALMANAC DETAILS AUSPICIOUS AND INAUSPICIOUS DATES AND SHOULD BE CONSULTED BEFORE ANY MAJOR CONSTRUCTION WORK BEGINS.

Personal Conduct and Feng Shui

In an ideal world everyone could choose the perfect site to build a house or to site a grave, but for the majority of people means and circumstance dictate the site. The feng shui expert can suggest ways to alleviate any misfortune associated with the site but cannot guarantee health, good luck or prosperity for the family. Some may be resigned to their fate and accept bad luck as a consequence of feng shui but the feng shui expert will not accept such fatalism.

Following the guidelines of feng shui is an aid to a prosperous and healthy life, but the most influential factor is personal conduct. It is said that a true and honest heart can overcome the misfortune associated with the most inauspicious of sites. We are born within a certain framework and are subject to parameters that are beyond our power to control, but a great deal of what we make of life lies in our own hands, which is why the Tao and the arts and sciences are there to guide us. The Chinese believe that if we can operate within the way of the universe then good fortune will follow. The following story illustrates this belief.

The Feng Shui Master and the Old Woman

Many centuries ago there was a feng shui master who was known for his skill but who was easily moved to anger. One hot summer he was commissioned to assess a burial site in the mountains far from his home.

It took him three days to walk to the site and a day to carry out his work. After sleeping in a small mountain shelter, he packed his compass and papers and set off for the long journey home. On the second day, he ran out of water in the overbearing heat, but as he surveyed the fields of rice ready for harvest that lay across the plain before him, there was no sign of a well.

In the distance, he saw a woman and three children working in the fields and so he headed in their direction. The woman stopped winnowing the long stalks of rice and her three sons lay down their scythes and baskets to stare at the stranger.

'Can I ask you for a bowl of water? I am exhausted and thirsty', said the feng shui master. 'I cannot walk any further without water'.

The woman crossed to a nearby tree, bent down and uncorked the pitcher of water that stood there. She poured clean, cold water into a wooden bowl, but before she handed it to the feng shui master she threw a small handful of chaff onto the surface of the water.

The feng shui master immediately felt anger welling up inside him and grabbed the bowl from the woman without a word of thanks. As he sipped the water, he continually had to blow the chaff to one side. He was convinced that the woman had insulted him, and as he emptied the bowl of water he thought of revenge.

'Do you live here?' asked the feng shui master.

'Yes, I live with my three sons in the hut at the far end of this field. My husband died two years ago and I have three sons to care for and feed. As you can see we are poor people.'

The feng shui master slowly gazed towards the hut and at the surrounding land. 'No wonder you have such bad fortune', he replied. 'I can tell you now that the feng shui of your house is unlucky. As long as you stay here you will only know misfortune, but I think I can help you. Beyond the other side of that mountain there is a plot of land and a dilapidated house. Although the land needs clearing and the house repairing, the feng shui is excellent. I suggest that you move there as soon as possible.'

The woman and her sons bowed down to the feng shui master in gratitude, and without reply he raised his bags over his shoulder and left them. In revenge for the chaff thrown on his bowl of water, he had directed them to 'Five Ghosts Dead Place', a site so inauspicious that the sons would be lucky to reach the age of 20.

Five years passed before the feng shui master returned to the area to see how the family had fared. As he approached the house the mother came out to greet him and bowed before him.

'Do you remember me?' he asked

'Of course I do. How would I forget your kindness. We followed your wise advice and you can see how my lands are fruitful. Two of my sons are studying for government jobs, my third son will soon be leaving to study with a wise teacher. Please come into my house and accept a meal.'

As the feng shui master sat eating the rice and vegetables offered by the woman he looked around in amazement at the newly plastered walls and the new furniture.

'How can this be?' he thought to himself, 'the site hasn't changed, there is still bad feng shui and she has no charms to protect herself.' 'I don't understand what has happened here,' he admitted to the woman. 'When I needed water, you gave me water, but instead of clean water you threw a handful of chaff on the surface to spite me. I therefore sent you to a site that had such bad feng shui you couldn't possibly have survived here, and yet your family is flourishing. What have you done that Heaven can bless you in this way?'

'Didn't you realize?' laughed the woman, 'it was a hot day, you had travelled a long way, and I knew you were exhausted. You were so thirsty that you would have swallowed the water in one go and the shock of the cold water would have been too much for you. You had to blow on the water to clear the chaff each time you took a mouthful, so you drank it more slowly. I was trying to protect you.'

The feng shui master nodded his head in recognition.

'Now I understand very well. I sent you to an evil place but your action has been rewarded. Every day Heaven and the Buddha will bless you.'

LIVING IN HARMONY

CHAPTER ONE

In Chinese philosophy, yin and yang are the two cosmic forces that shape and balance all life. They are opposites in a continual state of flux and tension, and it is through this dynamic that they produce life. Yin, which is feminine, luminous and fluid, is present in the moon, rain and floods. It is counterbalanced against yang, which is masculine, heavy and solid, the force that is in the sun, the stars and the earth. The forces of yin dominate as the cold and damp of winter approach, and wane as yang reasserts itself in the warmth and new growth of the early spring. Yin and yang are never represented as gods, nor are they associated with divine power – they are purely natural forces that were brought into being through the emptiness that existed at the beginning of time.

Feng shui is the way of divining yin and yang in the surrounding landscape. It is the art and science of reading a landscape so that homes for the living and dead can be sited where the balance of yin and yang is positive and where ch'i, the life breath, can circulate freely.

RIGHT THE NATURAL FORCES OF YIN AND YANG MUST BE IN HARMONY WHEN CHOOSING AN AUSPICIOUS SITE FOR A HOME OR A BURIAL.

The Creation of Yin and Yang

The creation of the two opposing, yet complementary, cosmic forces of yin and yang are described in the *Huai Nan Tzu* (circa 120 BCE), a study of natural philosophy recorded in 21 volumes:

Before Heaven and Earth had taken form, all was vague and amorphous. Therefore, it was called the Great Beginning. The Great Beginning produced emptiness and emptiness produced the universe. The universe produced material forces that had limits. That which was clear and light drifted up to become Heaven, while that which was heavy and turgid solidified to become Earth. It was very easy for the pure, fine material to come together but extremely difficult for the heavy, turgid material to solidify. Therefore Heaven was completed first and Earth assumed shape afterwards. The combined essences of Heaven and Earth became yin and yang. The concentrated essences of the yin and yang became the four seasons, and the scattered essences of the four seasons became the myriad creatures of the world. After a long time, the hot forces of the accumulated yang produced fire and the essence of the fire force became the sun; the cold force of accumulated yin became water and the essence of the water force became the moon. The essence of the excess force of the sun and moon became the stars and planets. Heaven received the sun, moon and stars while Earth received water and soil.

LEFT AND ABOVE ACCORDING TO ANCIENT CHINESE BELIEF, THE ACCUMULATED FORCES OF YANG BECAME FIRE, WHILE THE ACCUMULATED FORCES OF YIN BECAME WATER.

THE NATURAL LANDSCAPE

Feng shui, literally wind and water, is founded on the belief that the hills and rivers have been, and still are, eroded by the forces of wind and water. The term feng shui represents the power of the natural environment, which is alive with powerful hidden forces. By understanding the natural processes of the land and observing the patterns of change, a feng shui expert can discern favourable directions and good or malign influences at any place in the environment. Experienced in Chinese calendrical and natural philosophy, the expert can assess the landscape and recognize an imbalance in the forces of yin and yang, identify constructive or destructive movements between the five elements, or identify a blockage on ch'i, the life-giving force.

LEFT THE HILLS AND RIVERS OF OUR LANDSCAPE ARE ERODED BY THE POWERFUL NATURAL FORCES OF WIND AND WATER. A HEALTHY ENVIRONMENT SHOULD CONTAIN A BALANCE OF YIN AND YANG FORCES.

These principles are all central to the practice of feng shui but an expert will also give a detailed reading for any given site by consulting his or her Lo Pan compass. Each ring of the compass dial is inscribed with symbols that form a physical representation of the cosmos with its vast array of interrelated real and imaginary forces, phenomena and creatures (*see* Tools of the Geomancer, p.93).

Feng shui is a way of living harmoniously with, rather than conquering, the natural world. It is a model for dealing with reality, a means of positively aligning the fortunes of an individual or community with the Tao, or "The Way" – the inevitable, powerful and harmonious way of the universe.

THE ANCIENT SOURCES OF FENG SHUI

Feng shui dates back at least 3,000 years, although its philosophies and symbols have their origins in an even earlier period. The earliest reference to feng shui exists in the *History of the Former Han Dynasty*, which tells of the *Golden Box of Geomancy and Terrestrial Conformations for Palaces and Houses*. Unfortunately, neither book has survived. Two books that had a formative influence on the feng shui masters, and which are included in the *Imperial Encyclopedia*, are *The Burial Classics* by Kuo P'o (fourth century CE) and *The Yellow Emperor's Dwelling Classic* by Wang Wei (fifth century CE). The latter distinguishes between yin dwellings for the dead and yang dwellings for the living. Through the centuries more manuals have been written as guides to the siting of tombs for the deceased than for the siting of palaces, offices and houses for the living. This is because the well-being of the living depends, to a large extent, upon the appropriate burial and the continued care of their ancestors. A well-sited grave not only appeases the spirits of the dead, but also bestows good fortune upon their descendants. Feng shui manuals that focus upon sites for the living are, by contrast, more preoccupied with the immediate concerns and practicalities of everyday life.

THE TRADITIONAL ROLE OF THE GEOMANCER

Although feng shui was frowned on through the centuries by the sophisticated and practical Confucians, it was an essential part of Chinese existence, and most people at some time in their lives would have consulted a geomancer.

A geomancer was traditionally referred to as *feng shui hsien-sheng*, a title of great respect. Geomancers were treated with much deference, and were frequently carried to and from the site of their consultation in a sedan chair. They were employed on a part or full-time basis and traditionally received hospitality and gifts rather than monetary payment.

Besides being honoured for their literacy, geomancers were believed to possess insight into the mysterious working of nature and an understanding of powerful cosmic forces beyond the scope of the average citizen. They considered themselves scientists, and information on geomancy appears in the *Imperial Encyclopedia* under arts and divination, not under religion.

When a geomancer was present at a funeral he was there as a guide, familiar with the powers that shape this world. He prepared the ground for a priest who then stepped in to act as the intermediary between the land of the living and the land of the dead. The geomancer may only have been a consultant in this process but he was often held in awe and suspicion because of the power he wielded. His decisions could affect the fortunes of a family, so it was considered foolhardy to ignore his advice. However, it was difficult to prove incompetence if the family should suffer bad luck in the following years. If this happened, the family would once more call in a geomancer to assess the site and hopefully suggest a way to dispel the misfortune.

The geomancer could also prove to be divisive in family life. His decrees on the siting of a tomb could create family squabbles or litigation, and this unfilial conduct could in its turn disturb the harmony that should govern a burial. At times, the geomancer was a threat to the state itself. Ch'ing emperors are said to have taken precautions against families who had been predicted by a geomancer to form a new dynasty.

Although his knowledge is still widely respected and his pronouncements are taken seriously, the geomancer's judgement no longer wields the same power over ruling families or governments in modern day Chinese communities.

The Power of the Geomancer

There is a story told not only of the geomancers' questionable status but also of the secret forces they could summon up:

The Seven Star Peak is located in a place north of Ch'ao Ch'ing in Kuangtung province. To its west is a hill that closely resembles the back of a turtle whose head is formed by several large stones jutting out into the water.

A rich man summoned a geomancer who told him that 10 years ago the turtle opened its mouth, and that this unusual event was due to happen again on a certain day that year. He advised the wealthy man to bury the bones of one of his ancestors there.

And so the rich man took the coffin of one of his ancestors, placed it into a boat and, accompanied by the geomancer, they sailed to the site of the turtle rock. As they approached the whirlpool that lay close to the head of the turtle, the geomancer waited until the whirlpool gave a particularly loud roar and then ordered the rich man to push the coffin into the water. The rich man did as he was told, but no sooner had he disposed of the coffin than he began to regret his actions. He had failed in his duties to his ancestor by disposing of the body in an

unorthodox place. He accused the geomancer of trickery and deceit and took his case to a local magistrate. After hearing the evidence, the geomancer was ordered to return the coffin to the rich man. The geomancer asked the magistrate to lend him his sword and returned to the stone turtle. He climbed onto the turtle's back and, with a swipe of his sword, he sliced off the stone head and, by doing so, destroyed its power. The coffin resurfaced and the geomancer returned it to the rich man. When the rich man opened the coffin, he immediately regretted his decision – the body of his ancestor had become covered in golden scales.

ABOVE THE TURTLE IS A SYMBOL OF GOOD FORTUNE IN FENG SHUI AND APPEARS IN MANY ANCIENT CHINESE LEGENDS.

SYMBOLS OF HEAVEN AND EARTH

CHAPTER TWO

Feng shui divines the forces that are in Heaven and on Earth so that humanity can live in balance with them. Heaven, Earth and humanity share a mutual responsibility to maintain the harmony of the universe. Humans fulfil their role by understanding the cosmological forces of creation and by knowing how to be at one with their flow and change. The basic principles used to identify these forces in feng shui are the same as those that govern Chinese arts and sciences such as astrology, physiognomy and acupuncture. The most important principles are listed in the following pages.

The Five Elements

The five elements – water, fire, wood, metal and earth – are types of energy that are effective in all substances and changes. In any individual substance or phenomenon all elements are present in greater or lesser proportions. Feng shui practitioners believe that these five elements interact with each other in the physical world to create good and bad luck.

The elements are one of the ways in which Chinese philosophy relates to the growth and decay of the universe. The five elements are

ABOVE FIRE

ABOVE WATER

ABOVE METAL

ABOVE EARTH

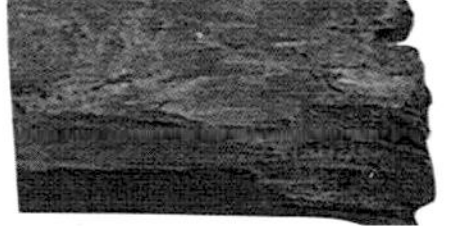

ABOVE WOOD

arranged in a highly systematized set of relationships whose origin cannot easily be traced. In the *Shu Ching* or *Book of History*, Heaven decreed the order of the universe in the 'Great Plan with its nine divisions'. The first of these divisions is the Five Elements: *'Of the five elements, the first is named water; the second, fire; the third, wood; the fourth, metal; and the fifth, earth. The nature of water is to soak and descend; of fire, to blaze and ascend; of wood, to be crooked and to be straight; of metal, to obey and to change; while the virtue of earth is seen in seed-sowing and in gathering. That which soaks and descends becomes salt; that which blazes and ascends becomes bitter; that which is crooked and straight becomes sour; that which obeys and changes becomes arid; and from seed-sowing and in gathering comes sweetness.'*

The five elements are the link that gives symbolic expression to the heavenly stems, earthly branches and the 24 points of the compass (*see* p.93), the astrological terms that mark out the divisions of time and space. Not only are the five elements a common reference for astrological observations and definitions, they are also a system to correlate everything in the universe that can be grouped into five, often on an arbitrary basis. The table on p.29 illustrates some of these correlations.

THE FIVE ELEMENTS AND THEIR DESTRUCTIVE OR PRODUCTIVE CYCLES

As is indicated in the 'Great Plan', the five elements have the power to create or destroy each other, thus giving rise to a new element. Their interaction is also an indication of the good or bad fortune that may befall a person or place. This is the order is which they produce or destroy:

wood produces fire

fire produces earth

earth produces metal

metal produces water

water produces wood

wood destroys earth

earth destroys water

water destroys fire

fire destroys metal

metal destroys wood

THE FIVE ELEMENTS AND THEIR CORRELATIONS

	WOOD	FIRE	EARTH	METAL	WATER
PLANET	JUPITER	MARS	SATURN	VENUS	MERCURY
COLOUR	GREEN	RED	YELLOW	WHITE	BLACK
TASTE	SOUR	BITTER	SWEET	ACRID	SALT
FIVE CLASSES OF ANIMALS	SCALY (FISH)	FEATHERED (BIRDS)	NAKED (HUMAN)	HAIRY (MAMMALS)	SHELL-COVERED (INVERTEBRATES)
YIN AND YANG	LESSER YANG	GREATER YANG	EQUAL BALANCE	LESSER YIN	GREATER YIN

The elements are also reflected in the shapes of hills and mountains and in the direction of watercourses. The main forms are illustrated in the box below and on p.30.

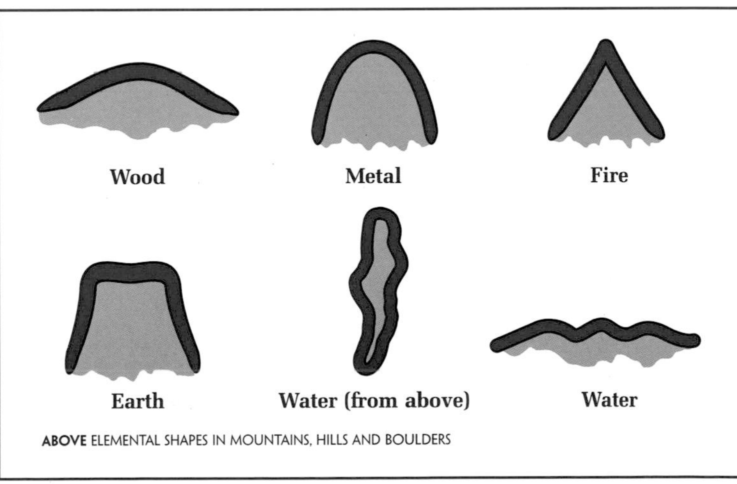

ABOVE ELEMENTAL SHAPES IN MOUNTAINS, HILLS AND BOULDERS

or

Wood

Metal

Fire

or

Earth

Water

ABOVE ELEMENTAL SHAPES IN WATERCOURSES

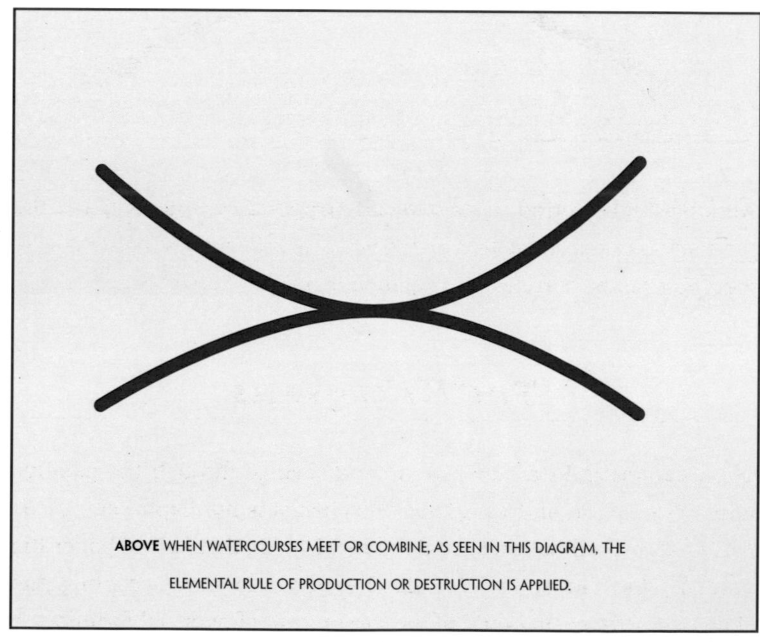

ABOVE WHEN WATERCOURSES MEET OR COMBINE, AS SEEN IN THIS DIAGRAM, THE ELEMENTAL RULE OF PRODUCTION OR DESTRUCTION IS APPLIED.

One fire or two woods entering a metal wall would indicate that the family will endure misfortune for many generations. Depending on the interpretation of the watercourse, fire destroys metal or metal destroys wood.

In the illustration below, water enters metal and since metal produces water the family can expect prosperity and honour for many generations to come.

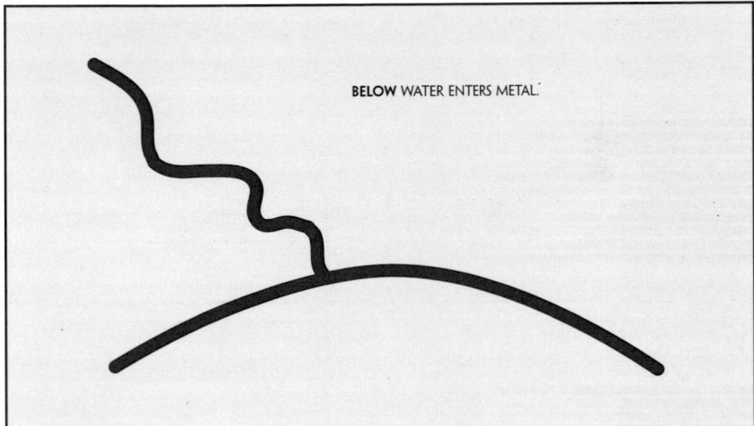
BELOW WATER ENTERS METAL.

Although not referred to directly on every ring of the compass, the geomancer can correlate the elements with each ring in the same way that they can be correlated to phenomena in the universe.

THE HEXAGRAMS

The universe is in a constant state of change through the creative interaction of yin and yang. But this change is not haphazard – it is part of an overall pattern, ordained by Heaven, that is the Tao, or the Way of the Universe. By following the Tao and accepting the changing patterns, not only of the seasons but of personal fortune, we

The Eight Trigrams

CH'IEN

The Creative

ELEMENT: BIG METAL

DIRECTION: NORTHWEST

NUMBER: 6

K'UN

The Receptive

ELEMENT: EARTH

DIRECTION: SOUTHWEST

NUMBER: 2

KEN

The Mountain

ELEMENT: EARTH

DIRECTION: NORTHEAST

NUMBER: 8

K'AN

The Abysmal

ELEMENT: WATER

DIRECTION NORTH

NUMBER: 1

The Eight Trigrams

CHEN

The Arousing

ELEMENT: WOOD

DIRECTION: EAST

NUMBER: 3

LI

The Clinging

ELEMENT: FIRE

DIRECTION: SOUTH

NUMBER: 9

SUN

The Gentle

ELEMENT: WOOD

DIRECTION: SOUTHEAST

NUMBER: 4

TUI

The Joyous

ELEMENT: METAL

DIRECTION: WEST

NUMBER: 7

maintain harmony with Heaven and Earth. If we fight change, we upset the balance between Heaven, humans and Earth and by doing so we are going against the Tao.

At the moment of creation, all things are given a specific nature by a principle called li. Li is order and it is expressed through the Tao. The order of every living thing is ordained at the moment of coming into being and it is the duty of all things to abide by li through correct and righteous behaviour. The importance of order is summed up in the following commentary from the *Ch'un Ch'iu – Records or Annals of Spring and Autumn*;

'"Allow me to ask," said Chien Tzu, "what we are to understand by ceremonies (li)". The reply was, "I have heard our late great officer Tzu Ch'an say, "Ceremonies are founded in the regular procedure of Heaven, the right phenomena of Earth, and the actions of men." Heaven and Earth have their regular ways, and men take these for their pattern, imitating the brilliant bodies of Heaven and according with the natural diversities of the earth. Heaven and Earth produce the six atmospheric conditions, and make use of the five material elements. These conditions and elements become the five tastes, are manifested in the five colours, and are displayed in the five notes. When these are in excess they ensure obscurity and confusion, and the people lose their proper nature. The rules of ceremony were therefore framed to support that nature."'

The essential resonance within the universe and the unceasing pattern of change within an ordered framework is reflected in the 8 trigrams and their 64 possible combinations.

The *I Ching*, or *Book of Changes*, probably dates back beyond the Chou dynasty and is the product of an ancient system of oral divination. The commentaries and appendices that accompany the 64 hexagrams of the I Ching were concluded by the Han dynasty. Tradition has it that the original hexagrams, known as the Former Heaven sequence, were formulated by Fu Hsi, the mythical bearer of the gifts of civilization. He is credited with the invention of the

LEFT ACCORDING TO ANCIENT CHINESE LEGEND, THE EIGHT TRIGRAMS FIRST APPEARED ON THE BACK OF A TURTLE SHELL THAT EMERGED FROM THE RIVER LO.

Chinese calendar and the civil administrative system, but he is best remembered as the bringer of the eight trigrams. One legend tells how he first saw the eight trigrams marked out on the shell of a turtle. (It is known from investigations at a Chou dynasty site that turtle shells inscribed with crude characters or signs were used for divination.) In turtle or tortoise shell divination, a small hole was made in the shell and heat applied until the shell cracked, and the lines that subsequently formed were then read by someone skilled in the art of divination. It is likely that these cracks were the inspiration for trigrams since shells have been found inscribed with lines, often three in number.

There is no indication of how or when the trigrams developed into hexagrams but by the early Chou dynasty the 64 hexagrams were in existence. Each trigram is made up of three lines. The line can be broken (- -) or unbroken (—). The broken lines are yin and the unbroken lines are yang. The eight trigrams reflect the gradual movement from absolute yin to absolute yang and back to absolute yin again in a never-ending cycle. When the trigrams are placed into pairs they form 64 combinations or hexagrams. The hexagrams and commentaries on each are recorded in the *I Ching*. A hexagram is chosen through the random selection of coins, throwing of yarrow sticks, bamboo sticks or, historically, through the appearance of cracks in a heated tortoise shell. It is by allowing random choice to govern the choice of hexagram that an individual is able to tap into the flow of the universe and be guided by the inevitable flow of the Tao.

THE FORMER HEAVEN SEQUENCE

In this sequence, line one, the innermost line, determines the trigram's cosmic force and sex, and the second line determines the extent of yin or yang, male or female, and, if the balance is still the same, then the third line is taken into account. For example, judging from the first line, Ch'ien, Tui, Li and Chen are yang and male; the remaining four are yin and female. Judging from the second line, Li is more male and yang than Chen since it has two unbroken yang lines

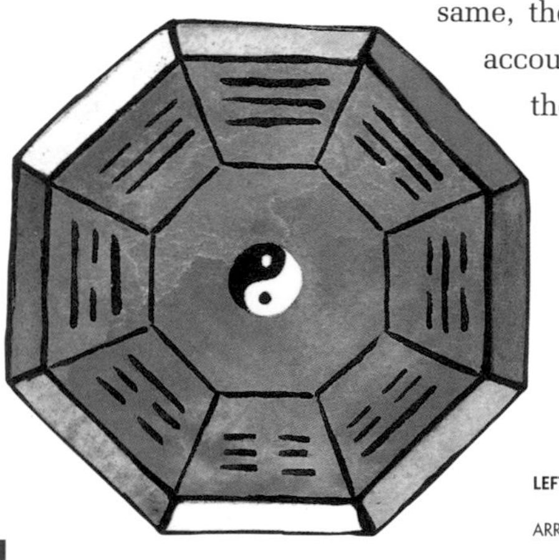

LEFT THIS PA KUA SHOWS THE FORMER HEAVEN ARRANGEMENT OF THE EIGHT TRIGRAMS.

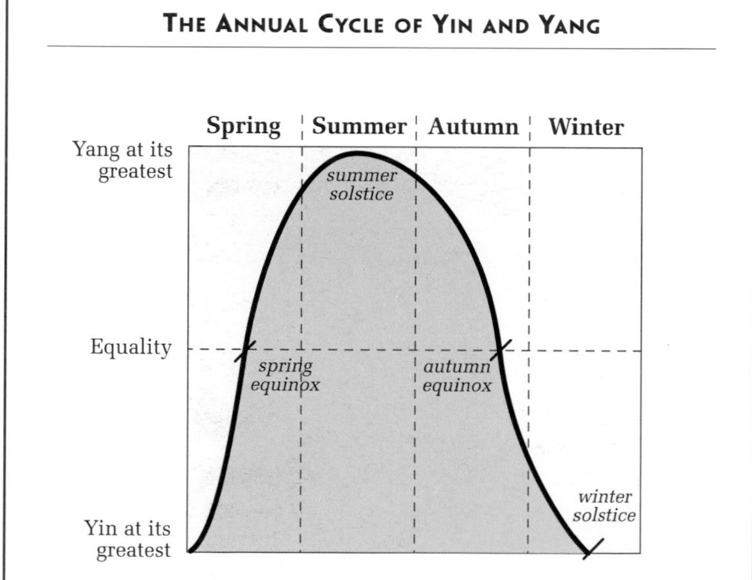

compared to Chen's two broken yin lines. The sequence itself represents the gradual accumulation of yin as it travels up the trigram to form absolute yin and then its decrease to allow for the accumulation of yang to form absolute yang and then the growth of yin again in each trigram.

The former Heaven sequence represents the annual cycle of yin and yang as they wax and wane through the seasons and enables the geomancer to relate to the forces of the cosmic yin and yang.

THE LATER HEAVEN SEQUENCE

The Later Heaven sequence is attributed to King Wen (circa 1160 BCE). Legend tells how he was captured by invading forces of the Shang dynasty and imprisoned for a year. During that time he wrote short and cryptic descriptions of each hexagram.

Many of his judgements consist of a few characters without pronouns or tenses. These judgements were elaborated on by his son, King Tan, who produced equally cryptic commentaries that are open to interpretation according to the diviner.

This sequence does not reflect the seasonal cycle of events but does reflect the points of the feng shui compass. The trigrams show the

RIGHT THIS PA KUA, KNOWN AS THE YANG PA KUA, SHOWS THE LATER HEAVEN SEQUENCE. IT IS USED TO SHOW YIN/YANG BALANCE ON THE GROUND.

Trigram Associations and Correlations for the Later Heaven Sequence

HEXAGRAM (LATER SEQUENCE)	NAME AND ATTRIBUTE	FAMILY RELATIONSHIP
CH'IEN	CREATIVE, STRONG	FATHER NW
K'UN	RECEPTIVE, YIELDING	MOTHER SW
CHEN	AROUSING, MOVEMENT	ELDEST SON E
SUN	GENTLENESS, PENETRATION	ELDEST DAUGHTER SE
K'AN	DANGER, FLOWING WATER	MIDDLE SON N
LI	ADHERENCE, DEPENDENCE	MIDDLE DAUGHTER S
KEN	STEADINESS, STILLNESS	YOUNGEST SON NE
TUI	JOY, SERENITY	YOUNGEST DAUGHTER W

HEXAGRAM	NATURAL PHENOMENON
CH'IEN	HEAVEN
K'UN	EARTH
CHEN	THUNDER
SUN	WIND
K'AN	MOOD
LI	SUN, LIGHTNING
KEN	MOUNTAIN
TUI	LAKE

balance of yin and yang at a particular spot on the ground. This reading is then compared with a reading from the Former Heaven sequence so that the cosmic yin and yang can be balanced with the localized yin and yang. By doing so the greater invisible forces of Heaven can be compared to the visible features on the land.

The commentaries and interpretations that accompany the hexagrams in the *I Ching* are not always relevant to the compass reading and are often used simply to inform the geomancer of patterns of change. The trigrams are important for direction, determining yin and yang balance, for their associations with symbols on the compass and for their correlation with anything else that can be formed into an eightfold group.

THE 60-YEAR CYCLE

The Chinese calendar revolves around a cycle of 60 years. The cycle is formed by the interaction of the 10 Heavenly Stems and the 12 Earthly Branches, which are units of time and place. Each year, a stem is paired with a branch and a new combination is produced so that the Heavenly Stems are repeated five times in this calendar and the Earthly Branches are repeated six times. In the first year the Heavenly Stem is Chia and the Earthly Branch is Tzu. Following the yearly rotation, this combination will take 60 years to appear again.

The branches, in particular, give information about time and place, although they are the means by which the heavenly bodies can express their influence. On the feng shui compass, the branches mark directions of the earth, and identify the ch'i of the earth, the dragon ch'i. The stems are associated with water and can be used to mark twists, turns and branches of watercourses.

When they stand on their own, the Earthly Branches correlate to the 12 animals of the Chinese horoscope, 12 months, 12 double-hours of the day, 12 directions and 12 groups of animals associated with the 28 constellations. The 12 animals of the Chinese horoscope do not

The 60 Year Cycle

HEAVENLY STEM	EARTHLY BRANCH
CHIA	TZU
YI	CH'OU
PING	YIN
TING	MAO
WU	CH'EN
CHI	SZU
KENG	WU
HSIN	WEI
JEN	SHEN
KUEI	YU

HEAVENLY STEM	EARTHLY BRANCH
CHIA	HSU
YI	HAI
PING	TZU
TING	CH'OU
WU	YIN
CHI	MAO
KENG	CH'EN
HSIN	SZU
JEN	WU
KUEI	WEI

HEAVENLY STEM	EARTHLY BRANCH
CHIA	SHEN
YI	YU
PING	HSU
TING	HAI
WU	TZU
CHI	CH'OU
KENG	YIN
HSIN	MAO
JEN	CH'EN
KUEI	SZU

HEAVENLY STEM	EARTHLY BRANCH
CHIA	WU
YI	WEI
PING	SHEN
TING	YU
WU	HSU
CHI	HAI
KENG	TZU
HSIN	CH'OU
JEN	YIN
KUEI	MAO

HEAVENLY STEM	EARTHLY BRANCH
CHIA	CH'EN
YI	SZU
PING	WU
TING	WEI
WU	SHEN
CHI	YU
KENG	HSU
HSIN	HAI
JEN	TZU
KUEI	CH'OU

HEAVENLY STEM	EARTHLY BRANCH
CHIA	YIN
YI	MAO
PING	CH'EN
TING	SZU
WU	WU
CHI	WEI
KENG	SHEN
HSIN	YU
JEN	HSU
KUEI	HAI

The Jade Emperor and the 12 Animals of the Chinese Horoscope

One day the Jade Emperor was bored of life in Heaven, and as he idly gazed towards the Earth he wondered what the creatures of that land looked like. Now that his curiosity was aroused, he summoned one of his assistants:

'Go down to the earth and order the creatures to come and visit me in the palace'.

'But there are so many, you majesty, do you want me to bring them all?' replied the assistant.

'No, I only want to see the most interesting. Select 12 and bring them to me as soon as you can.'

The assistant travelled to Earth and gave his first invitation to a rat. 'When you see your friend, the cat, ask him to come to the palace. I know the emperor will be fascinated by his coat.'

The assistant then continued on his journey and along the way he sent invitations to the ox, the tiger, the rabbit, the dragon, the snake, the horse, the ram, the monkey, the cock and the dog, telling them to be at the palace at six o'clock the next morning.

The animals preened themselves in preparation and the rat dutifully went in search of the cat. The cat was delighted to hear the news but since he was a deep sleeper, he made the rat promise to wake him up early the next morning. The rat gave his promise to the cat but the more he thought about the cat, the more jealous the rat became.

'That cat is far too beautiful, he will outshine me', he thought to himself. And as the night wore on the rat decided not to wake the cat as he promised.

The next morning 11 animals were lined up for inspection in the palace courtyard. The Jade Emperor walked slowly past each one

and when he come to the end of the line he turned to his assistant. 'They are fine creatures, but where is the twelfth one? I want the last animal here immediately', demanded the king.

Afraid that he may lose his position in the palace, the assistant returned to Earth at full speed to find a substitute for the cat. The first thing that caught his eye was a servant carrying a pig through a farmyard and so the assistant took the pig to the parade.

Meanwhile the rat was still anxious to be noticed and so he sat on the ox's back and played flute. The king was fascinated by this unusual creature and gave him first place.

The ox was placed second since he had been generous enough to allow the rat to sit on his back. The courageous-looking tiger was placed third and the rabbit with his fine white hair was placed fourth. The king thought the dragon resembled a strong snake on legs and so he was given fifth place. The snake was given sixth, the horse seventh, the ram eighth, the monkey ninth, the cock tenth and the dog eleventh. The king considered the pig the ugliest of all the assembled animals, and he had no choice but to give him the twelfth place.

No sooner had the king madke these awards than the cat ran into the palace.

'I'm sorry, your majesty, I overslept but I beg you now to give me a chance.'

However, it was too late, the king had already made his decision on the 12 animals of the horoscope and their corresponding 12 earthly branches.

The cat accepted his fate but he could never quite forgive the rat, and to this day the cat still bears that grudge.

correspond to stars or groups of stars as do the 12 animals of the Western zodiac.

The Chinese day is traditionally broken into 12 hours, each hour corresponds to two ordinary hours. The chart on p.44 shows how each animal of the Chinese horoscope was attributed a year, a time of day, a period within the year and a direction.

When the Heavenly Stems, Earthly Branches and four trigrams appear on the compass to mark the 24 directional points (*see* p.41), they are not only used for marking the positions of the dragon ch'i and of watercourses, but they are also used for marking lucky and unlucky points. The stems can be used as numerals 1 to 10. Stems 1, 2, 9 and 10 are unlucky; stems 3, 4, 7 and 8 are lucky. Stems 5 and 6 are at the centre of the compass and not on this directional ring. They are said to be unlucky but they are capable of dispersing the positive

ABOVE THE DRAGON CH'I (THE CH'I OF THE EARTH) CAN BE IDENTIFIED BY THE EARTHLY BRANCHES THAT APPEAR ON THE FENG SHUI COMPASS.

The Earthly Branches

EARTHLY BRANCH	ANIMAL	PERIOD OF THE YEAR	HOUR	DIRECTION
T-ZU	RAT	MID-WINTER	11PM–1AM	N
CH'OU	OX	END OF WINTER	1AM–3AM	NNE
YIN	TIGER	EARLY SPRING	3AM–5AM	ENE
MAO	RABBIT	MID-SPRING	5AM–7AM	E
CH'EN	DRAGON	END OF SPRING	7AM–9AM	ESE
SZU	SNAKE	EARLY SUMMER	9AM–11AM	SSE
WU	HORSE	MID-SUMMER	11AM–1PM	S
WEI	RAM	END OF SUMMER	1PM–3PM	SSW
SHEN	MONKEY	EARLY AUTUMN	3PM–5PM	WSW
YU	COCK	MID-AUTUMN	5PM–7PM	W
HSU	DOG	END OF AUTUMN	7PM–9PM	WNW
HAI	PIG	EARLY WINTER	9PM–11PM	NNW

The Heavenly Stems

HEAVENLY STEMS	NUMBER	DIRECTION IN THE 24 POINTS	LUCK
CHIA	1	ENE BY E	BAD
YI	2	ESE BY E	BAD
PING	3	SSE BY S	GOOD
TING	4	SSW BY S	GOOD
WU	5		
		CENTRE	BAD
CHI	6		
KENG	7	WSW BY W	GOOD
HSIN	8	WNW BY W	GOOD
JEN	9	NNW BY N	BAD
KUEI	10	NNE BY N	BAD

energy of ch'i over areas where malign forces have accumulated. The elements are placed at interim stages to indicate their interaction between the various aspects of the stems.

THE EIGHT CHARACTER HOROSCOPE

Before giving a reading of a site the geomancer must, at the very least, know the birth date of the person concerned. Using the Pa Che method (*see* chapter 3, p.52), their corresponding element, hexagram and auspicious directions can be calculated. For greater accuracy, he may produce an eight character horoscope using the stems and branches that correspond to the hour, date, month and year of birth. The days and months, like the years, follow a cycle of 60, and the stems and branches rotate accordingly. The stems and branches allocated to the hours follow a fixed pattern.

CH'I

Ch'i is commonly referred to as the life breath. The skill of the geomancer lies in his ability to allow for the unhindered circulation of this beneficial energy in relation to dwellings of both the living and of the dead.

The main purpose of ch'i is to function as the principle that shapes all forms. This function is described by the philosopher Chu Hsi:

'Throughout heaven and earth there is Li and there is Ch'i. Li is the Tao (organizing) all forms from above, and the root from which all things are produced. Ch'i is the instrument (composing) all forms from below, and the tools and raw materials with which all things are made. Thus men and all other things must receive this Li at the moment of their coming into being, and thus get their specific nature; so also must they receive this Ch'i and thus get their form.'

While li determines order, ch'i animates it so that it is capable of physical being – they are interdependent, one cannot exist without the other.

A feng shui expert is concerned with the place where ch'i accumulates, because this will bestow fortune on those who live or those who are buried there. When referred to in its plural form, ch'i is identified with yin and yang as they operate in the changing of the seasons, in the climate and in the landscape. Ch'i comes and goes in a continuous flow, prospering and dispersing, growing and decaying. The continual and often irregular accumulation and dispersal of ch'i at certain points on the ground is known as 'earth ch'i'. The stages of ch'i at any time or place on the ground can be identified by the geomancer using the information on the compass dial.

The ch'i that govern the regular cosmic cycle of seasons are known as 'heaven ch'i'. Besides the division of the year into four seasons, the annual cycle is broken into six phases, known as 'heaven ch'i'.

The six phases do not fall at regular intervals – according to the year some are more pronounced than others. The phases are further divided into 24 terms, which mark solar, climatic and agricultural patterns. These phases occur every 15–16 days, and are described in detail on p.104.

There is yet another aspect of ch'i that is related to the earth, but is not part of it in the same way as earth ch'i. This is ch'i in the literal sense of the life breath or energy that courses through the earth – the arteries and veins of the dragon – and through its rivers and streams. By observing the lie of the land, the geomancer can observe where ch'i are accumulating.

Shallow, fast-flowing rivers or streams disperse ch'i, as do hills exposed to strong winds. These are the places where yang accumulates. Low-lying valleys and pools of water encourage ch'i – they are sources of peace and quiet and a reflection of yin. This ch'i, which can be identified in the broad sweep of the landscape, is different to readings taken on the compass that identify ch'i at specific points on the ground.

ABOVE THE DRAGON IS ONE THE MOST IMPORTANT SYMBOLS OF FENG SHUI. BENEFICIAL CH'I IS KNOWN AS THE DRAGON'S COSMIC BREATH, AND THIS ENERGY RUNS THROUGH THE EARTH.

Ch'i produce life but they are also subject to decay and their absence or weakness in an area or spot will allow sha, the life-taking breath, to enter. Sha can appear as the result of one element overpowering or destroying another, causing sickness, business failure, family arguments, marital disputes or impotence.

Sha, in its physical sense, is manifest in the cold wind that blows from the earth through hollows in the land and in wind that pierces gaps in ridges or outcrops that protect a site. Sha that takes life and distributes malign influences can be found anywhere. This type of sha travels along a straight line, natural or made by human hands. A corner of a building facing onto a railway line, telephone line or straight watercourse is considered bad feng shui.

An ideal site is protected and peaceful but open to gentle winds that allow ch'i to circulate. This site should be south facing. A south facing site is particularly important in China since the site will benefit from warm, wet winds and will be protected from bitter northern winds.

A building or grave should be built in a hollow on a gentle slope so that air can circulate freely. The soil should be well-drained but not hard or rocky. A pool of water lower down the slope will not only improve drainage but will also encourage the accumulation of beneficial ch'i.

Details outlining the advantages and hazards of choosing building sites, domestic or commercial premises are outlined later in the book (*see* chapters 5–8).

The Ideal Grave Site

Chinese settlements and tombs still follow the ground rules of feng shui. The dead should be buried on a south facing slope, above the town and protected from malign spirits by mountains to the north. The good fortune resulting from the protection of the ancestors flows down the slope and into the town that, facing south, receives the benign influence of the summer sun. The city of Canton in southern China is a good example of this planning, and most Chinese towns will try to incorporate these basic elements as much for practical reasons as cultural ones.

Well-drained soil is also required for the preservation of the coffin, and, more importantly, for the preservation of the bones. Finding a site that affords good bone and coffin preservation is seem by the Chinese as a filial duty.

Besides the practical benefits, a well-placed site will bring good health, family harmony and successful trading. A site that is pleasing to the eye and peaceful to live in, which receives the sun and has an unrestricted view of natural features, will no doubt encourage emotional well-being.

Planning a Tomb

'Near the surface, one half should be sand and one half clay, with but few large stones. After digging four or five feet you may come upon a rick that cannot be moved, or upon water, and the place has to be abandoned. At a depth of three or four feet a layer of clay may be reached, and at six or seven feet a layer of sand, then a layer of loose stones, and then a layer of hard clay, yellow, red or variegated. Beyond this, water will be reached. Those buried above the hard clay find the air warm and comfortable, and have no trouble from water or white ants. Good clay is a sure indication that it is a safe place to bury, and the quantity of the clay may be tested by taking bits from the side and straining it through water. If no sand appears and the clay feels greasy to the touch, it is good.' (from B C Henry *The Cross and the Dragon*, New York, 1885).

THE PA CHE SYSTEM – A PERSONAL COMPASS

CHAPTER THREE

The Pa Che is an eight-sided symbol and is one of the main reference tools used in feng shui practice. Each of its sides corresponds to one of the eight compass directions (north-west, south-west, north-east, north, east, south, south-east and west). The centre is also considered one of the directions. The Pa Che system uses the later trigrams to determine the nine directions. The life of every individual will match one of these directions. The charts that appear in this chapter will enable the reader to discover his or her own favourable and unfavourable directions, thereby identifying the directions where good or malign spirits have particular influence. Once you have calculated the number of your compass there is a table that lists the colours most appropriate to your nature as well as the elements that can cause harmony or chaos is your life.

Pa Che feng shui is divided into two groups known as the eastern life and the western life. Each individual will belong to one of these groups. In an eastern life, southern, south-eastern, east and northern directions bring good fortune. In a western life, western, north-west, south-west and north-east bring good fortune. If, after making the calculations below, you discover that you have an eastern life, you should live in a eastern house. If your main door faces to the east you

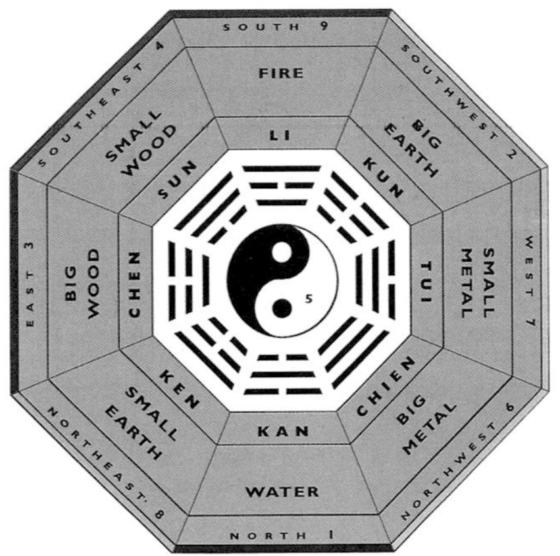

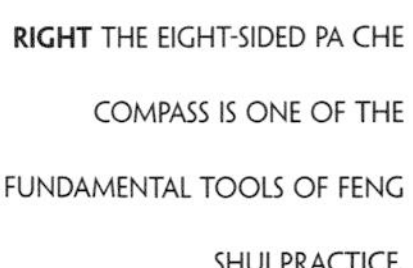
RIGHT THE EIGHT-SIDED PA CHE COMPASS IS ONE OF THE FUNDAMENTAL TOOLS OF FENG SHUI PRACTICE.

will have the most auspicious forecast. However, if these directions clash, then the harmony of your life will be disrupted.

Determining Your Own Pa Che Compass

In the following system, each one of the nine directions that corresponds to a trigram and to an element is given a number. These numbers, which are said to have been revealed through the mysterious forces of Heaven, are contained in the *Book of River-Lo* and the *Plan of the Yellow River.* Although there are only eight trigrams, there are nine directions, since the centre is considered one of the directions. In this system, K'un and K'en are repeated so that they align with the centre, which corresponds to number 5. If, after making your calculations, you end up with the number 5, you will discover from the compass illustrated above that the centre does not have its own particular forecast although it is an essential direction. A man who calculates the number 5 should follow the reading that corresponds to K'un, number 2 and a woman should follow the reading that corresponds to Ken, number 8.

How to Find Your Directional Number

Calculations for Men

Subtract your year of birth from 100 and divide by nine. The remainder is your number. If there is no remainder you must take the number 9.

Example: For a man born in 1960
100 –60=40 divided by 9=4 with a remainder of 4.

The reading is contained in the compass surrounding number 4.

Example: For a man born in 1955
100–55=45 divided by 9=5

Since there in no remainder the correct reading is found in the compass surrounding number 9.

Calculations for Women

Subtract 4 from your year of birth and divide by nine. The remainder is your number. If there is no remainder you must take the number 9.

Example: For a woman born in 1960
60–4=56 divided by 9=6 with a remainder of 2.

The correct reading is found in the compass surrounding number 2.

Example: For a woman born in 1949
49–4=45 divided by 9=5

The correct reading is found in the compass surrounding number 9.

As you can see from the diagram below, the traditional Chinese compass is laid out with South shown at the top, and North at the bottom. On the following page, the compasses will be shown with North at the top, according to normal Western compass usage.

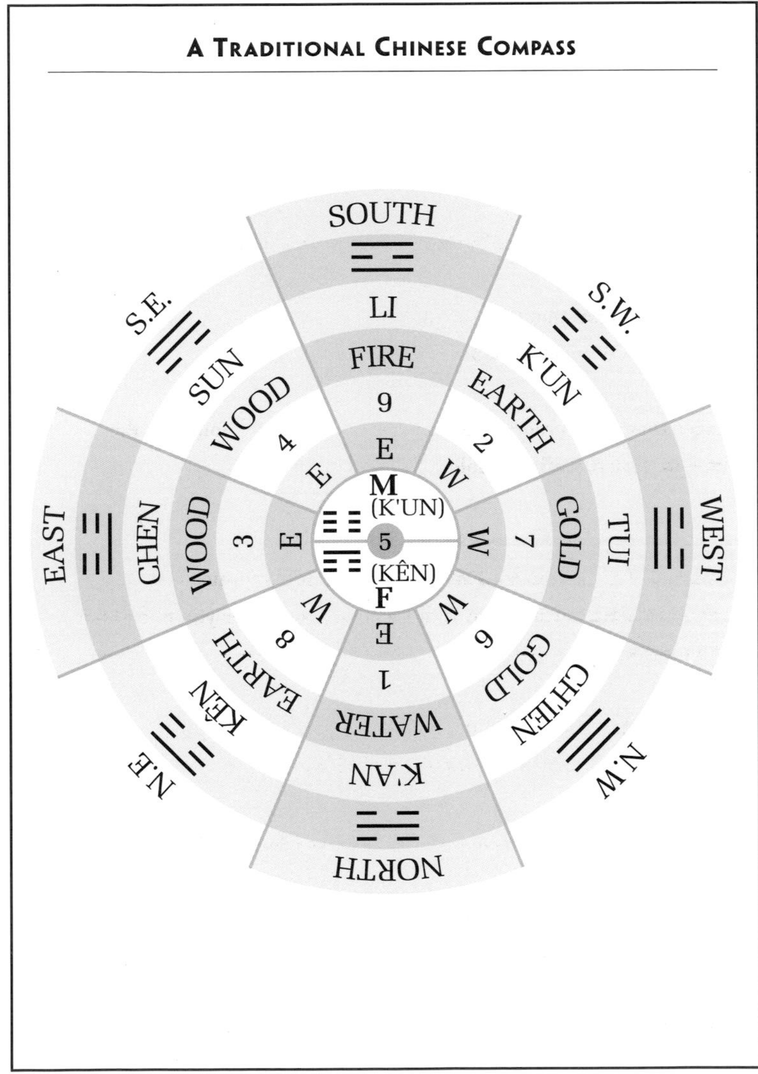

A Traditional Chinese Compass

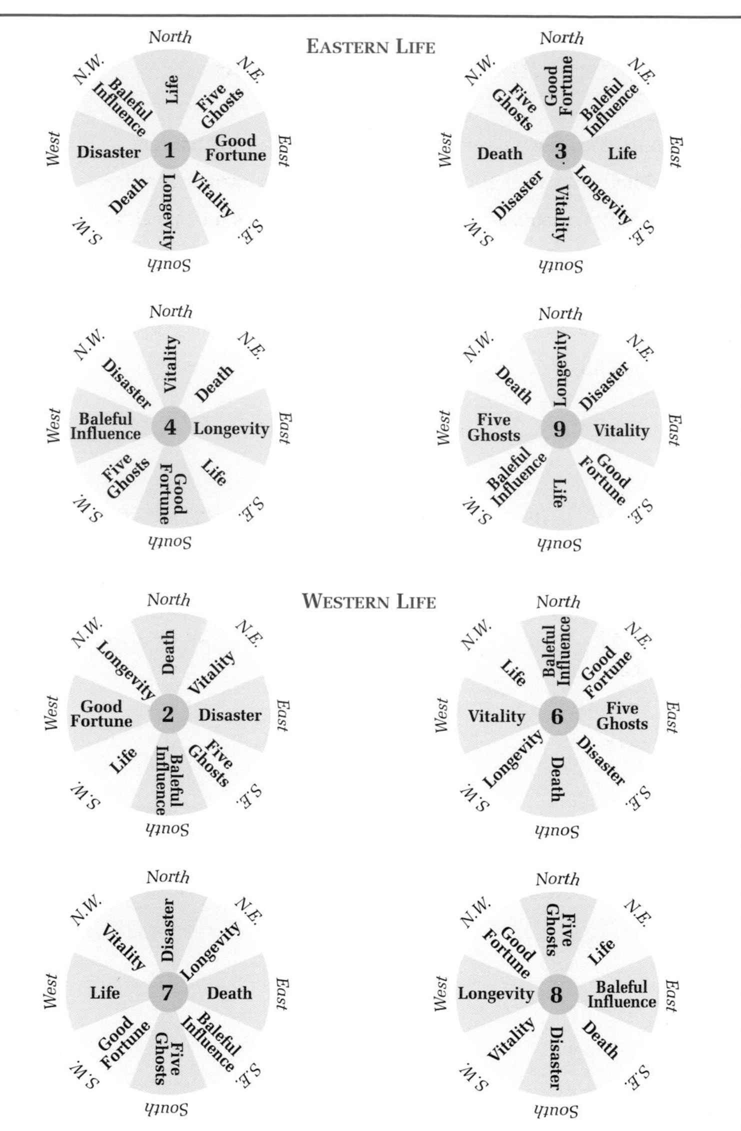

ABOVE VARIATIONS OF THE PA CHE COMPASS. ON A TRADITIONAL CHINESE COMPASS, SOUTH IS SHOWN AT THE TOP, BUT BECAUSE THIS BOOK WILL BE USED PRIMARILY BY A WESTERN AUDIENCE, THE COMPASS POINTS HAVE BEEN REORIENTATED ACCORDING TO NORMAL WESTERN USAGE.

UNFAVOURABLE DIRECTIONS

Not only does the compass give the reading for the trigram associated with your life, but each segment or direction of the compass represents a trigram. There are always four positive directions and four negative directions that apply to each individual. These different readings can help to explain the varying fortunes of a group of people who live and work in the same place.

UNFAVOURABLE DIRECTIONS FOR A WESTERN LIFE

ASPECT	TRIGRAM	ELEMENT
NORTH	K'AN	WATER
EAST	CHEN	WOOD
SOUTH-EAST	SUN	WOOD
SOUTH	LI	FIRE

UNFAVOURABLE DIRECTIONS FOR AN EASTERN LIFE

ASPECT	TRIGRAM	ELEMENT
SOUTH-WEST	K'UN	EARTH
NORTH-EAST	KEN	EARTH
WEST	TUI	GOLD
NORTH-WEST	CH'IEN	GOLD

Harmonious and Destructive Elements and Their Associated Colours

Once you have determined the number of your compass, its associated elements, trigram directions and influences, it is also possible to learn which elements and their corresponding colours work in harmony with your life and that bring misfortune. These is also a guide to help you determine auspicious and inauspicious directions, particularly when you are choosing a house.

Elements and Colours

WOOD (GREEN) IS IN HARMONY WITH FIRE (RED)

FIRE (RED) IS IN HARMONY WITH EARTH (YELLOW)

EARTH (YELLOW) IS IN HARMONY WITH GOLD (WHITE)

GOLD (WHITE) IS IN HARMONY WITH WATER (BLACK)

WATER (BLACK) IS IN HARMONY WITH WOOD (GREEN)

WOOD (GREEN) DESTROYS EARTH (YELLOW)

EARTH (YELLOW) DESTROYS WATER (BLACK)

WATER (BLACK) DESTROYS GOLD (WHITE)

GOLD (WHITE) DESTROYS WOOD (GREEN)

Finding a Suitable Home

Once you have found a house suitable for your feng shui reading, it is important to make sure that the position of the front door does not weaken your reading.

You can check that the position of the house and the position of the front door are aligned by using your appropriate model of the Pa Che feng shui compass created above. Stand at the centre of the house and hold the north point of the compass to the direction of the North Pole. If your feng shui falls into the eastern life group, the main door of your house should be at the north, east, south-east or south. If your feng shui falls into the western life group the main door of your house should be a the west, north-west, south-west or north-east.

MOUNTAINS, TREES AND RIVERS

CHAPTER FOUR

According to the principles of feng shui, a dwelling that is in harmony with its natural surroundings will prove lucky for its inhabitants. Auspicious locations include elevated or hilly land with gently meandering waterways.

MOUNTAINS

Mountains and other raised features of the land are yang. Full of secret cosmological meaning to the geomancer, these features also protect the site. An ideal site is situated on a slope, open to the south and protected from evil influences by mountains at the north. A pinnacle or point on the top of the mountain range is not auspicious, however, since it will allow the beneficial ch'i to be dispersed too rapidly by wind. Similarly, a fast running stream on the mountain slopes or at its base will also threaten the site.

Steeply flowing waterfalls are inauspicious, and steep mountain peaks will provide an excess of yang. A site that is low-lying among small hills or pools is also undesirable as it is a source of excess yin and a likely place for sha to accumulate. A high mountain range as a backdrop is acceptable for the site, provided there are foothills in front so that the excess yang caused by towering peaks is lessened. A headland jutting out from a horseshoe shaped mountain is a good choice of site, as is a peninsula or headland jutting out from the centre of a forking formation. This type of headland is sometimes referred to as the dragon's head. Two gently flowing streams should join together in front of the site and then flow away to the sides, preferably out of sight. On a well-chosen site, these streams or waterpool would be well drained and situated on a flat piece of land known as a Court Altar or Table.

TREES

In the absence of mountains, trees can have the same protective role provided that they are at the back and to the side of the house and not situated at the front. Well-established verdant tress, preferably evergreen, are a source of yang and are likely to bring good fortune. The tree should not be cut or scarred since this will detract from its beneficial influence. One well-sited evergreen tree is often more important than a grove of trees and is sometimes referred to as a feng shui tree.

ABOVE HEALTHY TREES BRING GOOD LUCK AND OFFER PROTECTION AGAINST HARMFUL CH'I.

WATER

Great attention is paid to the courses of streams and rivers in feng shui. They are one of the most easily identified natural features of the landscape and occur on both high and low land. The twists, bends and branches of a river are known as the Water Dragon as opposed to the Mountain Dragon. The various formations of a watercourse are given a feng shui interpretation in the *Water Dragon Classic*, which appears in the *Imperial Encyclopedia*.

The place where two rivers meet is a positive site, since influences are concentrated here, but a branch in a river often indicates a dispersal of positive forces. A sharp bend in a river is unlucky, since it forms straight, arrow like lines. A meandering river, by contrast, is considered a natural route of good influence.

WATER DRAGON CLASSIC

According to the famous *Water Dragon Classic*, an ideal site should nestle among watercourses so that it is protected in the stomach of the dragon.

'If water pours (away from the site) it drains off, it is hurried. How can it be abundant and wealth accumulate? If it comes in straight and goes out straight it injures men (Secret Arrow). Darting left, the eldest son must meet with misfortune; darting right, the youngest meet with calamity.'

Ch'i flows through watercourses and the branches that immediately surround a site and protect it are called inner ch'i, whereas the main trunk of the river that surrounds the site at the outermost point carries the outer ch'i. Outer ch'i is capable of nourishing the inner ch'i, which in turn penetrates gently into the house or grave. These general classifications are further defined by the shape of trunks and branches, by the sharpness of their bends, and by the arrangement of their shapes.

The illustrations on pp.63–65 assess favourable and unfavourable sites for a house.

Favourable Positions for a House

RIGHT THIS HOUSE IS PROTECTED BY THE BELLY OF THE DRAGON AND IS IN AN EXTREMELY AUSPICIOUS SITE .

ABOVE AND BELOW THE BLACK DOTS IN THESE FOUR ILLUSTRATIONS INDICATE FAVOURABLE SITES FOR A HOUSE. THEIR AUSPICOUS LOCATIONS WILL ENSURE THAT THE INHABITANTS OF THE HOMES ENJOY GOOD FORTUNE AND HEALTH.

Bends and Branches in Rivers and Streams

The directional flow of rivers and streams is interpreted through the eight trigrams and their influence. The following table indicates the fortune that can result from sharp bends or branches at various compass points.

Sharp bend at

N	CHILDREN WILL BE THIEVES, A RICH FAMILY WILL BECOME POOR
NE	NOTHING WILL BE LEFT FOR POSTERITY, CHILDLESS WIDOWS
ENE	DISEASE
E	GENERATIONS TO COME WILL BE POOR AND HOMELESS
ESE	DISOBEDIENCE

Branching at

NE, NW, SE, OR SW	PROSPERITY
ENE, WSW, SSE OR NNE	POVERTY, AND DISPERSAL OF OLDER SONS AND BROTHERS
E BY W, W BY S, S BY E, N BY W	HAPPINESS FOR CHILDREN
N BY E AND DUE W	UNHAPPINESS FOR CHILDREN

UNFAVOURABLE POSITIONS FOR A HOUSE

In the diagrams below, the dot represents the house and the surrounding lines are watercourses. These are unfavourable positions for a house.

Favourable Positions for a House

In the diagrams below, the dot represents the house and the surrounding lines are watercourses. These are favourable positions for a house.

SITE OF POSTERITY, WEALTH AND FAME

SITE OF GOOD FORTUNE

SITE OF POSTERITY AND WEALTH

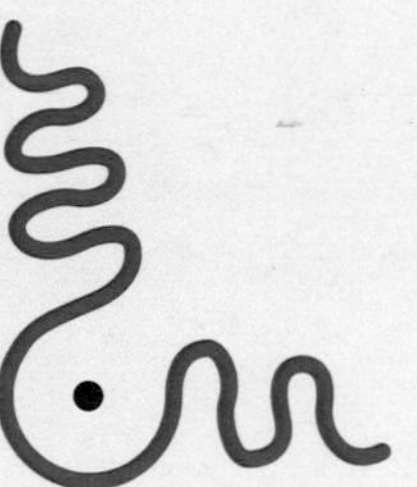

SITE OF POSTERITY, FAME AND FORTUNE

SITE OF WEALTH AND PROSPEROUS WELL-BEING

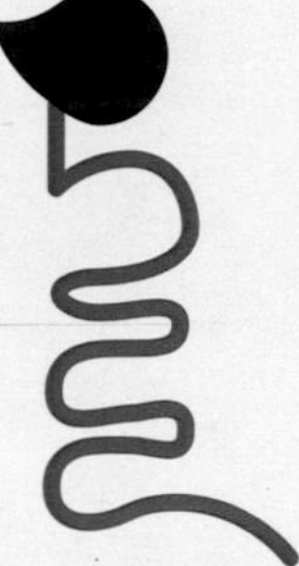

SITE OF POSTERITY AND WEALTH

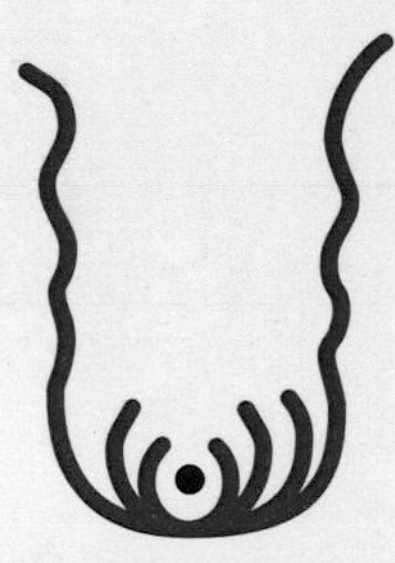

SITE OF GREAT WEALTH AND POSTERITY

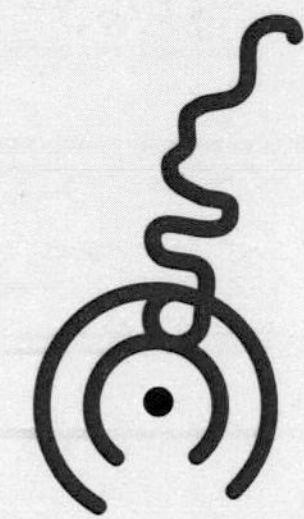

SITE OF POSTERITY AND WEALTH

SITE OF POSTERITY

SITE OF FAME

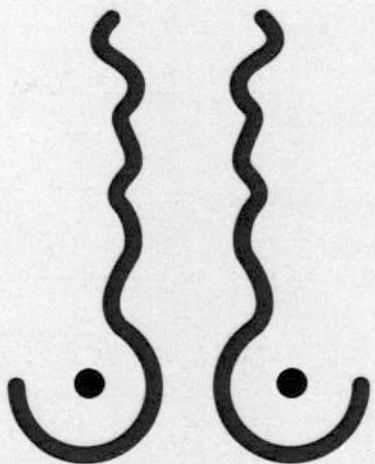

SITE OF GREATNESS

SITE OF POSTERITY, FAME AND FORTUNE

BUILDING OR BUYING A HOUSE

CHAPTER FIVE

When you plan to buy or build a house, it is important to examine first the site of the house, the surrounding buildings and the natural features of the land. According to the fifth century Chinese text, *The Yellow Emperor's Dwelling Classic.*

'A good earth will grow exuberant sprouts, a house with good fortune will bring prosperity.'

The Four Animals

Every house is surrounded by four animal spirits whose position is fixed around the front door of the house. As you face outwards from the main door of your house, the Green Dragon is at your left-hand side, the White Tiger is on your right-hand side, the Red Bird can be found at the front of the house and the Black Tortoise at the back.

The four animals represents orders of animals – the Tiger represents mammals, the Dragon represents fish, the Tortoise represents invertebrates and the Red Bird represents birds.

Their colours are also linked with the elements – green with wood, white with gold, red with fire, black with water while the house at the centre is the earth.

ABOVE THE FOUR CELESTIAL ANIMALS WILL PROTECT A SITE IF THEY ARE POSITIONED CORRECTLY.

In addition to symbolizing the animal kingdom and the elements, these semi-mythical creatures also represent the four quarters of the sky – north, south, east and west – which are linked with the four seasons – winter, summer, spring and autumn respectively. As well as standing on four sides of a site, the four animals can be identified by topographical forms, in particular through the courses of rivers or streams (*see* pp.68–69).

THE FOUR CELESTIAL ANIMALS AND WATERCOURSES

The Dragon is seen in a watercourse that has one bend or branch off from the main course. A site situated in this bend can bring wealth, honour and happiness.

The Tiger is seen in a river course with two of three branches. A site positioned in these branches, embraced by the Tiger's water, promises wealth and good fortune for future generations.

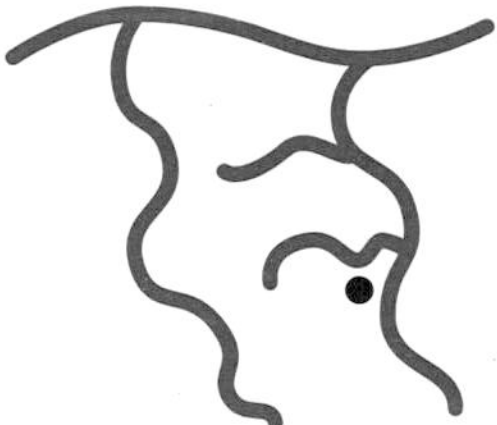

The Tiger is dangerous when two parallel streams turn and branch out. A site located in between their two divergent courses is likened to a tiger holding a corpse in his mouth and heralds poverty and childless old age.

The Red Bird is seen in watercourses that have three back turns. Sites positioned in these turns will be troubled by hunger and poverty. It is believed that men living here will be thieves and that women will be coarse.

The Tortoise is recognized by the loop resulting from the division of the main watercourse. This forecasts office and domestic happiness.

The Ideal Living Site

The *Yang'chai Shih Shu* or the *Ten Writings on Yang Dwellings* describes the conditions needed for an ideal living site:

'All dwellings are very honourable that have on the left flowing water, which is the Azure Dragon, on the right a long path, which is the White Tiger, in the front a pool, which is the Red Bird, and behind hills, which are the Sombre Warrior.'

Choosing the Ideal Site

The Green Dragon and the White Tiger to the left and right of the house can be likened to guards that must balance with one another. You should always make sure that there is an even balance between the left and the right-hand side of the house. For example, an extension built on the right-hand side of the house, extending into the front garden could herald disaster, since the White Tiger is too powerful for the Dragon to control. It is believed that the White Tiger will emerge to harm those in the house. When the animal spirits are in balance it follows that the forces of yin and yang and the elements are in balance.

On an ideal side, the front of the house is at a lower level than the rear of the house, the Red Bird is lower than the Black Tortoise. A garden that slopes upwards from the front door or steps that lead up from the front door could cause financial and domestic problems. High land at the back of a house protects the house and also provides you with support from family and friends. A back garden that is larger than the front will also offer support and protection. By contrast, if you have a larger front garden you are likely to miss good opportunities that come your way and in times of trouble you are unlikely to find help from your friends.

DAMAGE TO YOUR DIRECTIONS

These are the possible problems that could result from damage in one or more directions of your land.

EAST – could adversely affect the health of the eldest son and bring him misfortune.

SOUTH-EAST – damage in this direction could have a detrimental effect on women in labour and will generally bring bad luck to all women who live in this house.

NORTH-EAST – could bring illness to the youngest son or grandson.

SOUTH-WEST – the mother or eldest woman in the house will be prone to stomach upsets.

NORTH-WEST – the father or eldest male will be prone to lung disease or high blood pressure.

WEST – the youngest girl is likely to suffer from poor health.

SOUTH – the second daughter will be prone to brain disease and the daughters-in-law will encounter general misfortune.

NORTH – there will be general health problems in the family and the second son will be prone to accidents.

The majority of Chinese Buddhist temples and shrines are built on a flat piece of land, square in shape. Ideally, the same rule should apply to houses. See the box on p. 71 for possible problems resulting from damage to the directions of your land.

If the house was originally built on a square plot but a corner of the land has collapsed, been eroded or later used for another construction, illness or misfortune in the family may result.

If the front garden of the house is narrower than the back garden the family will enjoy prosperity and praise since the energy is focused in the area that supports the house, and there will be unexpected opportunities to further a business.

If a house is built on a triangular plot so that the front of the house faces the point of the triangle, everyone living in the house is likely to suffer from ill health. If the position of the house is reversed, fatal illness or suicide may result. Anyone buying a triangular plot of land is advised to buy additional land or to sell part of their land, in order to soften the triangular edge.

For practical health and structural reasons you are advised against buying property that has been built on reclaimed wetlands or dumping sites.

Try to choose a house that has been built close to others and in a regular pattern so that the ch'i can move smoothly from building to building. Ch'i has difficulty passing through scattered houses and irregular planning.

A house should always be at the same height or higher than those directly opposite and slightly lower than those behind so that ch'i can circulate, the houses behind can protect and pressure from taller buildings to the front can be avoided.

A half-moon shaped pond or pool to the front of the main door will encourage wealth, an unexpected windfall and general good fortune.

Prosperity and respect can be expected if the rear of the house is square and the front of the house round, for example, bay windows on either side.

Try to choose a property with a greater depth than width to

encourage happiness and stability in the home. If the width of your house is greater than its depth, the residents may suffer from mental illness or breathing difficulties.

With the exception of swimming pools, avoid building or buying a house with a pond or pool in the back garden since there will be an excess of yin spirits. If you do have a pond, you can help to reestablish the balance of yin and yang by planting osmanthus, magnolia or mechilia. Avoid planting azaleas or banyan trees.

Finally, avoid houses with inner courtyards since this is known as a 'Heaven Well' and the yin spirit is too strong. This area should be used to build living or sleeping accommodation.

FENG SHUI IN THE HOME

CHAPTER SIX

An auspicious home will be of great benefit to you and your family, bringing good fortune, health and happiness. Before buying a house, check that it is in balance with the surrounding environment, and that beneficial ch'i can flow freely. In this chapter, we will look at some of the main considerations to take into account when you buy your home.

The Main Door

One of the most important features is the position of the main door. The main door is subject to more traffic than any other part of the house. It is the door that protects the house, and is the means by which destructive spirits can enter the house and one of the ways lucky stars can spread their influence. In general, it is believed that a well-placed front door will encourage health, wealth and long life.

The main door should always be well-hinged, upright and in scale with the size of the house. If the main door is unusually large, it is said to cause a dent in the house, and the residents are likely to encounter financial difficulties. If the main door is comparatively small, the residents will be prone to petty arguments. The door frames are regarded as the supporting poles of the family and they

LEFT AN AUSPICIOUSLY PLACED MAIN DOOR WILL BRING GOOD LUCK AND PROSPERITY TO THE INHABITANTS OF THE HOUSE.

should be straight and free of rot. If the frame is bent or weak, the family's fortunes will suffer. It is advisable to place two lamps outside the front door. However, if one of the bulbs stops working it is considered a bad omen, and should be replaced immediately. Lamp-posts that stand in the garden are regarded as guardians of the house. Again, if the bulb of the post is damaged remember to replace it immediately. You should, however, avoid placing a lamp-post directly outside the main door of the property since this could cause financial loss.

Avoid planting trees directly in front of the main door since the strong yin nature of the tree not only blocks the yang entering the house but also sends additional yin inside.

The main door should not face the corner of another house since this corner is likened to a dagger stabbing the main entrance to your home. It will encourage ill-health and financial loss. The main door

BELOW THE MAIN DOOR OF ANY HOME SHOULD BE PROTECTED AGAINST HARMFUL CH'I FROM OPPOSING STRUCTURES.

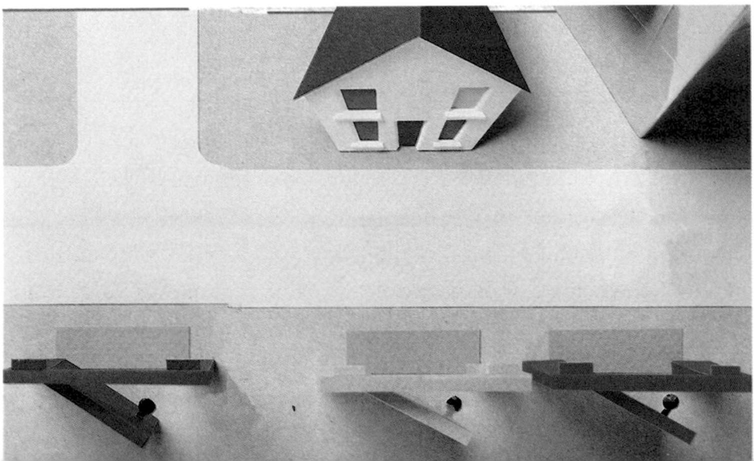

should never face a ‘dead end’ as the ch’i will be unable to circulate, and, like still water, the energy will stagnate and sha accumulate. Family life is likely to degenerate slowly into petty squabbles that arise from continually walking into the malign forces surrounding the house. From a practical point of view, a dead end can also make an escape difficult in case of fire.

If you are building a house you should place the main door towards the left-hand side, the Green Dragon side, so the dragon can exert his energetic spirit over the house. It is acceptable to place the main door in the centre, but unless your horoscope dictates the direction of the White Tiger you should avoid the right-hand side of the house.

Before buying a house, ensure that the neighbouring building on the right-hand side is not taller or larger than your potential home. Although this is good feng shui for the neighbouring house, it is bad feng shui for you. The spirit of the White Tiger at the right-hand side will outweigh the spirit of the Green Dragon on the left as he does not have the power to control the White Tiger.

ABOVE MAKE SURE THAT YOUR HOUSE IS NOT HEMMED IN BY BUILDINGS THAT ARE TALLER THAN YOUR HOME.

The main door of the property should never face directly onto a Y-shaped road or path since each time you leave the house you are faced with a choice of direction. This choice will eventually cause misfortune in your family or at your place of work.

Yin Spirits

The main door should never face directly onto churches, temples, monasteries or cemeteries. These places are full of yin spirits and it is believed that they are the refuge for homeless ghosts, souls and unknown spirits. It is, however, acceptable to buy a house with side or back walls facing religious buildings or cemeteries.

ABOVE THE RESTLESS YIN SPIRITS THAT INHABIT RELIGIOUS BUILDINGS AND CHURCHYARDS CAN HARM THE INHABITANTS OF ANY HOME THAT OVERLOOKS THEM.

Beware of a main door that faces a narrow gap between two buildings, which is likened in feng shui to a slice that has been cut out of a cake, and it could cause the family's savings to be slowly frittered away.

Walls or fences built around the house will create protective and beneficial feng shui provided that the fences are not too close to the house itself. The protective power of the feng shui is lost if the walls are less than two meters from the house.

ABOVE A HOUSE THAT IS SITUATED AT THE BEND OF A FLYOVER WILL SUFFER FROM BAD FENG SHUI.

A main door that faces a mountain or a hill could result in work difficulties or business loss. You should also avoid buying a house built on a steep hillside and facing a deep valley since this could cause mental illness. The feng shui of a house located in the bend of a stream, river or flyover will encourage ill-health and accidents in the family. The watercourse or road is likened to a blade stabbing at the house. From a practical point of view, it is believed that damp air blowing in from the water will cause arthritis or influenza.

Correcting Bad Feng Shui

If you do have a house that has bad feng shui, it is possible to place mirrors at strategic points to divert the malign influences. If, for example, there is a tree directly facing your front door, you should place a feng shui mirror surrounded by the eight trigrams above the door frame. This will deflect the bad feng shui. If a second feng shui mirror is considered necessary, choose one without the eight trigrams and with small indentations on the surface of the mirror. If the mirrors are needed in the same place, position the indented mirror on top of the trigram mirror and fix both to the wall above the frame of the door. These mirrors cannot, however, deflect the feng shui caused by a house facing a fork in the road, a dead end or a valley.

LEFT IF THERE ARE ANY UNLUCKY STRUCTURES FACING YOUR HOME, HANG A PA KUA MIRROR ABOVE YOUR FRONT DOOR. THIS WILL PROTECT YOU AGAINST ANY BAD FENG SHUI.

LEFT GOLDFISH ARE EXTREMELY AUSPICIOUS CREATURES TO HAVE IN YOUR HOME, AND WILL INCREASE THE FLOW OF BENEFICIAL CH'I.

The Sitting-Room

The master bedroom, kitchen and sitting-room are the three most important sites for positive feng shui in the house. Since the sitting-room is the area where family and friends gather, it is best situated on the ground floor, within easy access of the main door. It is, however, bad feng shui to have a straight view of the sitting room from the main door. If this happens, you should try to position a piece of furniture in an appropriate place to obscure part of this view. This rule does not, however, apply to a small sitting-room. Here you should attempt to create more space by hanging a mirror. Be careful, however, that the bottom steps of the staircase are not reflected in the mirror.

When you are positioning furniture do not place a sofa directly under a visible beam since this will put pressure on whoever is supporting the family. If there is no other place for the furniture, you are advised to have a false ceiling put in to hide the beam. Avoid a cluttered sitting-room as this blocks the flow of the ch'i. It is far better to have paintings or ornaments hanging on the walls than to have them placed on tables or on the floor. An aquarium containing goldfish will also help increase the flow of ch'i in your house.

LEFT SOFAS SHOULD NEVER BE PLACED UNDER A VISIBLE BEAM AS THIS WILL BRING MISFORTUNE TO THE HEAD OF THE FAMILY.

The most important point in the sitting-room is known as the wealth point, and it is situated on the top left-hand corner as you enter the room. It is believed that a door or a doorway beneath this point will encourage your money to seep away. A kettle or coffee-maker will also encourage your money to evaporate. If you are suffering from financial problems you are advised to grow a plant with large rounded green leaves in this position since the growth of the plant will reflect an upturn in your income. The larger the plant, the greater the fortune. Any dying leaves should be cut away immediately since this is a bad omen. It is also advisable to place three coins wrapped in red paper under the pot. However, you should avoid azaleas or other plants with sharp, pointed leaves as they attract negative forces and are therefore inauspicious. An artificial plant can improve the feng shui in this corner but only a fresh plant can provide the energy and power to attract positive forces.

LEFT AND RIGHT A HEALTHY PLANT WITH LARGE ROUNDED LEAVES WILL ENOURAGE MONEY TO ENTER YOUR HOME.

THE BEDROOM

Since almost a third of our time is spent in bed the feng shui of the bedroom, particularly the master bedroom, is very important. The position of the bed can have a major effect on health, prosperity and marriage. You can take a general feng shui reading on the position of your bedroom and bed if you stand at the centre of your house and use the Pa Che compass. However, the more attention that you pay to

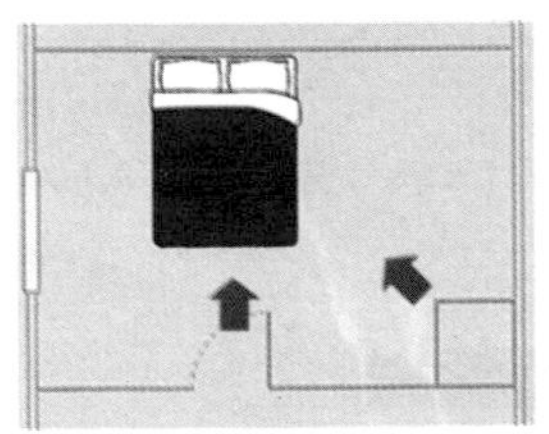

ABOVE NEVER PLACE A BED DIRECTLY OPPOSITE THE BEDROOM DOOR. THIS IS BAD FENG SHUI AND WILL DRAIN THE ENERGY OF THE BED'S OCCUPANT.

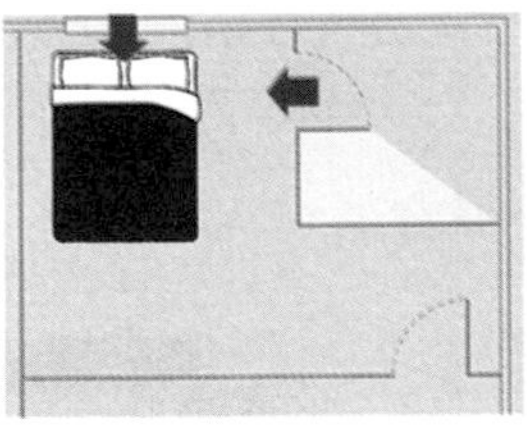

ABOVE NEVER POSITION A BED NEAR TO A WINDOW. THIS IS VERY UNLUCKY AND WILL CAUSE THE SLEEPER TO DEVELOP LIVER PROBLEMS.

ABOVE A BED SHOULD NEVER BE PLACED DIRECTLY UNDER A VISIBLE BEAM AS THIS WILL CAUSE HEADACHES AND MENTAL PROBLEMS.

the positioning of furniture in your bedroom, the greater your fortune.

The base of the bed should be on wheels, never in contact with the flow since this will prevent air from circulating and eventually cause damp in the bed and resulting backaches. Do not store articles under the bed as this will also cause ill-health. Never set the head of the bed towards the west unless you are advised to do so in your horoscope. This is particularly logical advice to those who live in the East since the western side of the house is always the hottest side.

Never set the head of the bed behind the bedroom door so that only the foot of the bed can be seen when the bedroom door is open – this will result in restless nights. The bed should never be directly opposite the door since this will drain away your energy. If a bed is positioned too close to the window, thunderstorms will cause restlessness, wet weather may encourage damp and in the long term this positioning may cause liver damage. The bed should never be placed directly under a visible beam since this will provoke headaches, mental disorders and loss of creative energy. A beam that crosses over the width of the bed, that is over your stomach as you lay in bed, will cause digestive problems. If the beam crosses over your legs and feet, it will cause swelling in your lower body and problems in your career. To avoid accidents, the bed should never be more than 3ft off the ground. Never position a bed directly opposite a mirror. This may frighten you should you awake suddenly and may also lead to nervous disorders.

If the bedroom is big enough it is easy to follow the rules above, However, if the bedroom is small you should follow the traditional Chinese system for setting a bed so that yin and yang are correctly balanced. If you were born in the summer, the head of the bed should face north to the cool spirits; if you were born in the winter, the bed should face south to the warm spirits. If you were born in the spring or autumn months, use the Pa Che system to determine your favourable direction.

Bedside lamps should not be fitted onto the wall directly above the head. If they are, then a low wattage bulb should be used. Very bright overhead bulbs not only damage eyesight, but it is believed they could eventually cause liver disease. A bulb that has blown should be quickly replaced as this a bad omen for the future. Avoid leaving hand mirrors or make-up sets on a dressing-table directly opposite the foot of the bed as they could have the same effect as a wall mirror in this position. Do not position a dressing table directly opposite a door since this causes bad temper and emotional problems. A dressing-table that is positioned directly under a beam will create a feeling of general ill-health.

The bedroom door should never face directly onto a kitchen or lavatory door since the steam and other vapours emitting from these rooms will cause sickness and could have a detrimental effect on the family's fortunes.

Decorate your room with colours that correspond to your elements in the Pa Che system. It is best to paper or paint the walls in light colours but if you prefer strong, dark colours then choose patterns that have a light background.

THE KITCHEN

A good feng shui reading for the position of the kitchen and the cooker will encourage good health, family prosperity and harmony, particularly for the housewife. The most favourable positions for the kitchen or cooker are the southern or eastern side of the house. The element of fire is linked with the south and the element of wood with the east. These directions are chosen for an eating area since wood is traditionally needed to produce fire for cooking. In ancient China, the majority of stoves were built on the eastern side of the house, and since the majority of the houses faced south it would have been unlucky feng shui to have the cooking area directly opposite the main door. Since wood and charcoal were the two main sources of fuel the south-easterly winds that blew across China were useful for igniting fuel. These were also the two coolest directions and therefore the most suitable places to store food.

ABOVE THE KITCHEN DOOR SHOULD NEVER FACE THE BATHROOM.

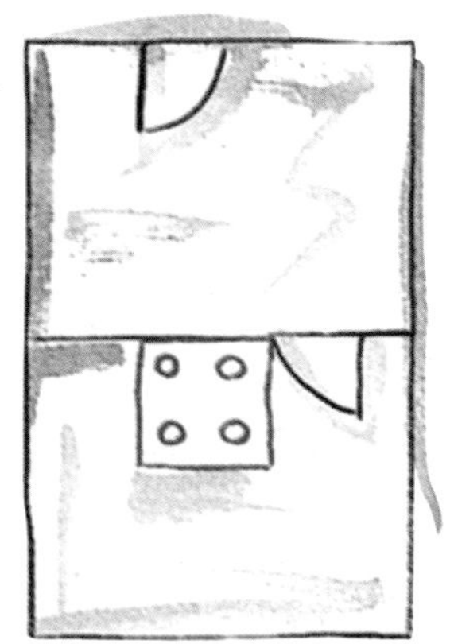

ABOVE IT IS CONSIDERED UNLUCKY FOR THE COOKER TO FACE THE MAIN DOOR.

The kitchen should be square or rectangular, never triangular. To avoid strong smells or steam entering other rooms, the kitchen door should never directly face onto other rooms.

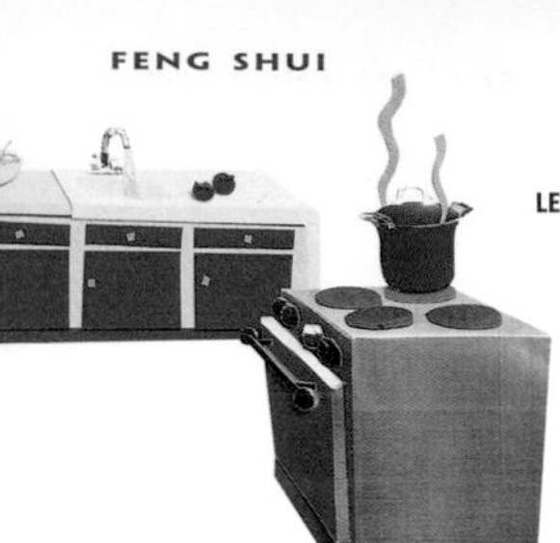

LEFT NEVER POSITION THE COOKER NEXT TO THE KITCHEN SINK. IF THEY ARE PLACED NEXT TO EACH OTHER, THIS WILL CAUSE THE ELEMENTS OF FIRE AND WATER TO CLASH.

The kitchen is regarded as a 'treasure', so if the doors at the front or back of the house face the kitchen door then good fortune can easily seep out of the house. A kitchen door that faces a living room will encourage bad health and arguments and a kitchen that faces a bathroom and lavatory will encourage the spread of germs. You should also check that the plumbing from the lavatory does not run under the kitchen floor.

The cooker should not be set next to a washing basin or close to a sink. If the cooker is next to the sink or refrigerator the elements of fire and water will clash. If the cooker is next to the window, wind can extinguish the gas or sun spoil the food.

It is traditional in many Chinese homes to have a small shrine to the kitchen god set close to the cooker. It is believed that he guards the kitchen, listening to any arguments, looking out for good deeds and making note of mistakes. On the 23rd day of the twelfth month he travels to Heaven to report to the Jade Emperor, the ruler of Heaven. Traditionally a family smears his lips with honey and burns joss-sticks in his honour to ensure a favourable report.

The Bathroom and Lavatory

The bathroom and lavatory can be built at any side of the house but never in the centre since the odours will spread throughout the house. Do not build a bathroom close to the main door of the house since the excess of yin spirits in this room will clash with the yang spirits coming through the main door.

LEFT KEEP YOUR TOILET AWAY FROM THE CENTRE OF YOUR HOME, AND ENSURE THAT IT IS NOT TOO CLOSE TO THE FRONT DOOR.

Shrines in the Home

If there is enough space, Chinese and Buddhist families will choose a room close to the centre of the house to build a shrine. If the space is limited, the family will usually place statues and offerings on a shelf in a quiet, clean corner of the house. There should always be an odd number of statues placed in hierarchical order. The Buddha should be placed in the centre with bodhisattvas standing on either side. Kwan Ti, the god of wealth, should be placed to the right of the bodhisattvas and a photograph of the ancestors should be placed to their left. If there is only one statue, for example, Kuan Yin, goddess of mercy, it should be placed in the centre. The shrine should be fixed on an auspicious day chosen form the T'ung Shu, the yearly almanac. The height of the shelf or table on which the statues are placed should be measured with a feng shui ruler. Finally, the shelf or table must not face the lavatory or kitchen door, or be placed under exposed beams.

ABOVE RELIGIOUS STATUES SUCH AS THIS ONE OF THE BUDDHA ARE OFTEN FOUND IN CHINESE HOMES.

LEFT IN FAMILY SHRINES, ANCESTRAL PHOTOGRAPHS ARE COMMONLY SITUATED TO THE LEFT OF THE BODHISATTVA STATUES.

FENG SHUI AND BUSINESS

CHAPTER SEVEN

The Chinese art of feng shui can be used successfully by those in business to ensure profits and to create a sound business environment. The rules that govern houses are mostly the same as those that govern shops or offices. You are, however, warned not to choose a shop or office building that combines several shapes in its ground plan. A professional geomancer would say that the quality and pricing of the goods on offer and a good business address can only partially compensate for a site or shop interior that has bad feng shui. Many of the feng shui principles used in the home can also apply to the place of work, although there are several additional features that should be taken into account.

LEFT MANY SHOPS DISPLAY A STATUE OF THE GOD OF WEALTH TO ATTRACT FINANCIAL SUCCESS TO THEIR BUSINESS.

Choosing a Shop

Choose an area with a dense population, even if there are many other shops in the area. Look for premises built on higher ground to avoid flooding in heavy rains and do not build or choose a shop at a lower level than the neighbouring buildings since good fortune will drain away. Make sure that the paving or garden area in front of the premises is smooth, clean and well-tended since awkward access will deter customers. The level of the shop floor should also be higher than the level of the road.

THE SHOP INTERIOR

The main entrance of the shop should be wider and higher than domestic premises. Since the house is a private place a small entrance helps to encourage a restful atmosphere, but the opposite should apply to a shop. It should be spacious and welcoming to avoid a sense of pressure. The design and colour of your front door is one of the major factors in determining your business fortune. It is the feng shui of the door that will attract the casual passer-by. The Chinese say that it is the spirit of good fortune coming from the door that attracts customers into the shop, even if, at first glance, there is nothing in the shop they particularly need.

After entering the main door, pay particular attention to any inside doors that directly face you; they should never be larger than the front door as they will exert too much control over the positive spirit of the front door. The Green Dragon is the most fortunate side for the main entrance since the active spirit associated with it will attract business. If the whole of the shop front is given over to an entrance, then make sure that access is through the Green Dragon side. Avoid creating access on the White Tiger side since this is traditionally the quiet side. If the spirit of the White Tiger is disturbed, he will symbolically react by devouring those who enter. In practical terms, this will herald accident or disaster.

One of the strict feng shui rules that applies to business or domestic premises is that the main door

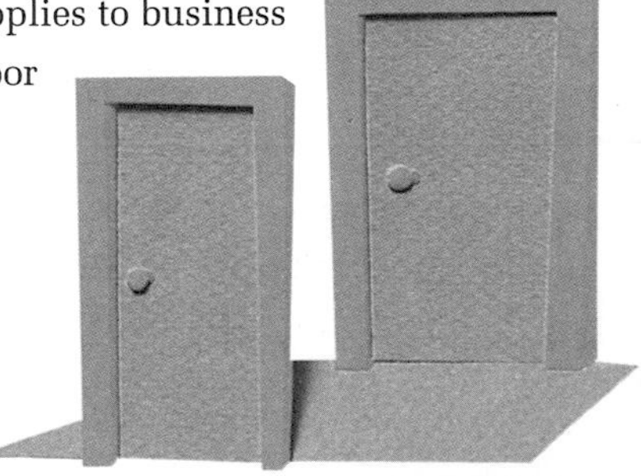

RIGHT INTERNAL DOORS SHOULD NEVER BE LARGER THAN THE MAIN ENTRANCE AS THEY MAY DETRACT FROM THE POSITIVE SPIRIT OF THE FRONT DOOR.

LEFT THE FRONT DOOR OF A BUSINESS SHOULD NEVER OPEN DIRECTLY ONTO A STAIRCASE AS THIS WILL ENCOURAGE WEALTH TO LEAVE THE PREMISES.

should never face the corner of another house or apartment building. This corner represents a dagger ready to stab the facing building. At home this position would cause accident or sickness and at work it will result in long term profit loss. If this positioning is unavoidable, the danger can be averted by fixing a screen inside or outside the door so that the entrance to the building is moved slightly to the side and the bad fortune is blocked.

The main door should never open directly inwards towards a staircase since it will force the wealthy spirit out into the street. This stems from the belief that the staircase is the route that ch'i takes to circulate the house and it could easily be misdirected through an open door into the road.

The main door should not open towards the direction of a lavatory since the yin spirit of this room will rush headlong into the incoming yang spirit from the main door. This sudden clash of opposite spirits is likely to cause illness and misfortune.

If the business premises has a kitchen or cooking facilities, these must never be seen by someone entering the shop since this could be the cause of fire. This rule does not apply to restaurants or cafes since cooking is at the centre of the business.

The main door should not face temples or churches since the Chinese believe that homeless ghosts and yin spirits dwell in these buildings. These restless spirits will not, however, disturb premises that sell religious statues or artefacts.

As with domestic accommodation, the main door must not face a mountain and the back of the premises should never face a valley or the sea. To avoid debt, make sure that the main door does not face a fork in the road. A main door facing a stream or a river will cause personal sickness as well as a loss in profits.

The main door should not face an outer bend in a flyover or bridge. The angle of the road can be likened to a sickle cutting into your profits. If, however, the shop faces towards an inner bend, this is likened to your premises being wrapped in a jade belt and, therefore, promises great wealth. It is important never to choose a shop that has an entrance facing the bottom end of a cul-de-sac since there is no escape for the malign spirits that become trapped in the road.

Always keep the main entrance and the area in front of it clean. You should also make sure that there are no exposed drainpipes since this will not only block the path of the wealthy spirits as they try to enter the house but it will also drain away the good fortune. The best place for drainpipes is at the back of the premises so rainwater is channelled away from the front of the shop. The Chinese believe that drains at the front of the house will also cause your capital to drain away.

FENG SHUI IN THE OFFICE

The feng shui of a business is largely determined by the position of the accounts office, cash register and the manager's office. The accounts should be reckoned on the White Tiger side of the office; since money is yin in nature it should be matched to the quiet nature of the tiger. The money should be kept in a quiet, concealed and safe place away from windows or doors or mirrors.

LEFT IF YOUR HOME AND BUSINESS ARE LOCATED IN THE SAME PLACE, MAKE SURE THAT YOU HAVE SEPARATE TOILETS FOR THE TWO AREAS. ALSO, NEVER POSITION A TOILET ABOVE THE MANAGER'S OFFICE OR THE ACCOUNTS ROOM.

It is advisable not to have living accommodation and office space in the same building but if this is unavoidable you should make sure that there are separate lavatories for the two areas. If the accommodation is above the shop, the first floor lavatory should never be positioned above the manager's room, the accounts office, the cash till or any statues or photographs that you respect as this will cause accidents or illness at work. If you run a cafe or restaurant, the cooking area should always face south or east.

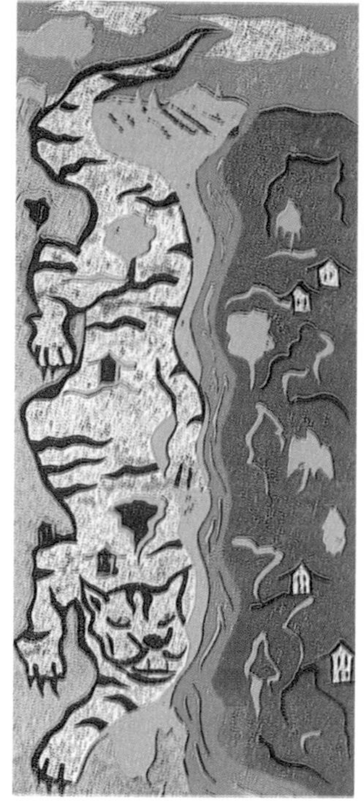

ABOVE THE ACCOUNTS ROOM SHOULD BE ON THE WHITE TIGER SIDE OF THE OFFICE.

THE DESK

The desk is the most important item of furniture in the manager's room. The desk should always be in a quiet place away from the public eye unless you have to entertain clients. It should be placed against a wall, which is likened to a strong mountain offering support and protection. The manager's back should never face windows or doors since the force of the ch'i is too great. This is known in feng shui as the 'empty door' and implies lack of support, concentration and power. The height of the desk should correspond to the 'wealth' and 'prosperity' markings on the feng shui ruler. The desk should never be placed under an exposed beam since this exerts too much pressure, nor should it be set at an oblique angle to the shape of the

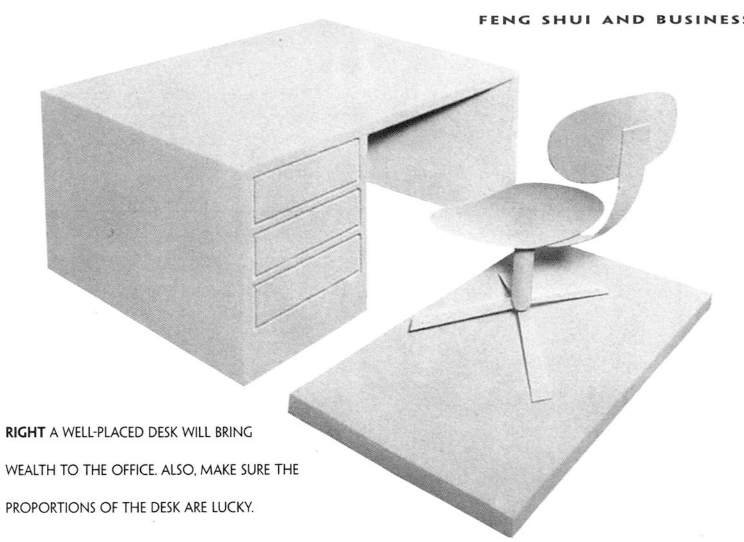

RIGHT A WELL-PLACED DESK WILL BRING WEALTH TO THE OFFICE. ALSO, MAKE SURE THE PROPORTIONS OF THE DESK ARE LUCKY.

room itself. This will only encourage financial setbacks and staff disagreements. A desk placed in one of the corners opposite the door will encourage healthy profits provided it does not clash with the directions of your horoscope.

Other desks in the office should be placed in regular rows around this main desk to allow for free movement.

PLANTS AND PAINTINGS

If your feng shui life corresponds to Li or Chen, represented by the elements of fire and wood, you are advised to keep several large-leaved green plants in your office. If your feng shui life corresponds to Ken or K'un you should keep the amount of greenery to a minimum, since wood is capable of destroying earth. Two plants at the office door and one plant at the wealthy point will be sufficient. The plants could be replaced by photographs or paintings.

RIGHT HEALTHY BROAD-LEAVED PLANTS SHOULD BE PLACED AT THE OFFICE DOOR AND WEALTH POINT TO ENCOURAGE GOOD FENG SHUI.

An office devoted to education is suited to landscape paintings in soft colours. Brightly coloured paintings of waterlilies, peonies and the large bloomed flowers (except azaleas), are suitable for an office that deals with trade. Police and military offices need stark and regular designs. Black and white calligraphy is well-suited to this environment. Offices that are concerned with the media are allowed more freedom with their choice of colour and content. However, in all cases it is important not to crowd the walls with too much detail or to fill the room with too many plants.

AQUARIUMS

An aquarium containing goldfish is an effective way of combating malign influences and converting negative spirits to positive spirits. There should always be an odd number of fish and the tank should be placed in one of the unlucky directions for your feng shui life.

THE TOOLS OF THE GEOMANCER

CHAPTER EIGHT

This introduction to the Lo Pan compass is based on a simple nine-ringed compass that contains the basic information a geomancer may need. To give an accurate reading, the geomancer correlates the symbols and information given in each ring with the horoscope details of the individual.

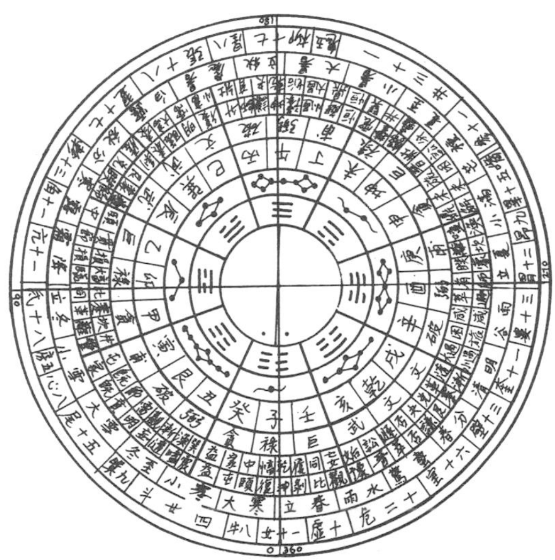

ABOVE THE LO PAN IS A SPECIALIST COMPASS USED BY THE FENG SHUI EXPERT. IT IS DIVIDED UP INTO RINGS, EACH OF WHICH CONTAIN SYMBOLS. IN A CHINESE COMPASS, SOUTH IS ALWAYS PLACED AT THE TOP OF THE COMPASS.

LANDSCAPE FEATURES

The symbols inscribed on the compass ring are rarely static since the forces in the landscape are in a continual state of flux. The symbols reflect the carefully balanced relationship between Heaven and Earth, the tension and opposition between yin and yang, the elements, hexagrams, stars, and the hundreds of other symbols of the compass. Even within a single series of symbols, one symbol refers to another and interacts with it. In practical terms this constant interaction is applied to the following five basic landscape categories:

SHAN

This is the dragon, the most important feature of the land since it can create or destroy human fortune. The dragon is linear in that it links every shape in the landscape to a line of other shapes. The twists, turns and curves of its body can be seen in all topographical formations. Hills, mountain ridges and formations are the dragon's veins and arteries through which ch'i, the dragon's blood, can circulate. Watercourses are the dragon's ducts through which the water ch'i can flow.

As with a human body, the dragon's body also has capillaries and ducts that carry ch'i but if there are too many small channels around a site the ch'i is easily dispersed. The higher the concentration of ch'i through the veins or arteries, the greater the fortune bestowed on the site. The geomancer can identify where the dragon's influence enters or leaves, disperses or leaks, condenses or collects. He is also able to determine the type of dragon – whether it is straight, lying across a site or riding a site. The point at which the forces in the landscape have a powerful and positive effect is called the dragon point.

SHUI

Shui refers to watercourses or pools flowing through, or situated close to, the site. Sluggish or stagnant water can affect the fortune of the site since it is a place where sha will accumulate. The quality and the movement of the water is also an indication of the soil type in the area.

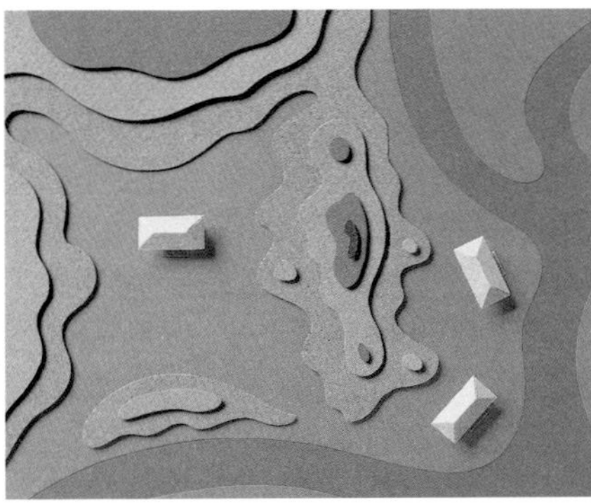

LEFT SHUI IS THE TERM USED FOR WATER IN THE LANDSCAPE. CLEAN AND NATURAL FREE-FLOWING WATER CAN BRING GOOD LUCK TO THOSE WHO LIVE NEARBY.

SHA

Sha is the term for formations of earth, mud or sand and is a term applied to unusual land or riverbank formations.

CHAI

Chai is the term used for the site itself or the dwelling, whether it is a house, tomb or office.

HSUEH

Hsueh is the 'lair' of the dragon. It also refers to the site, particularly if it is in a well-protected place such as a hollow or a site shielded on three sides.

LEFT YIN AND YANG INTERACT WITH EACH OTHER IN THE HEAVEN POOL, WHICH APPEARS IN THE CENTRE OF THE COMPASS AND IS REGARDED AS THE CENTRE OF THE UNIVERSE.

To take the bearings of a site or a feature of the landscape, the geomancer holds the compass or places it against the straight side of an object aligned with the direction from which he wishes to take the reading. The compass is set on a square base to make this possible. There are two threads held taut that cross at the centre of the compass and the geomancer positions the compass so that one of these threads is directly in line with the direction he is facing. The dial listing the concentric circles is moved around until it is aligned with the needle. A reading can then be taken along the line of symbols that appear under the line of the thread.

The centre of the compass is known as Heaven's Pool, or Tai Chi. The Heaven Pool is regarded as the centre of the universe. The area is divided in half by a magnetic needle. It is believed that the compass provides order for life and in the middle is the well of the Heaven Pool where action and rest work together. The Heaven Pool symbolically represents the starting point of ch'i, the life breath. It is in this pool that the forces of yin and yang can divide and interact with other – when one ascends, the other declines – and so they work and rest in harmony. Their action in turn gives rise to the elements and other forms and forces.

The first ring contains the original trigrams devised by Fu Hsi (*see* pp.32–33). The Former Heaven trigrams are laid out among the eight points of the compass. Within this sequence, the forces of yin and yang wax and wane. Yang is at its greatest in Ch'ien, the southern and most male trigram, and yin is at its strongest in K'un, the northern and most female trigram. This movement from strength to weakness through the trigrams of the Former Heaven sequence represents the cycle of the seasons from winter, when yin is at its peak, through spring and onto summer, when yang is at its peak and then the yin forces build up again through autumn to culminate in winter.

The Nine Stars Reflected in Hills and Mountains

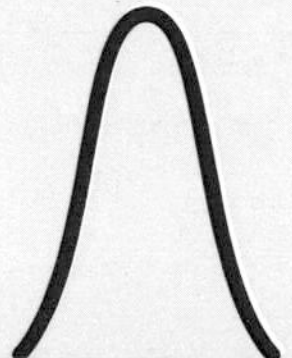

COVETOUS WOLF

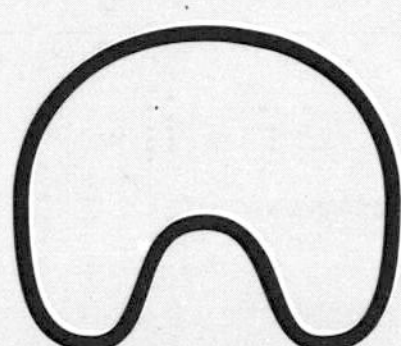

CHIEF GATE

PURITY AND TRUTH

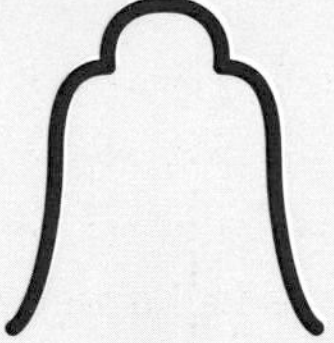

SALARY PRESERVED

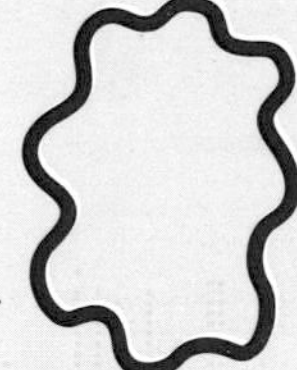

CULTURAL ACTIVITIES

(RAISED LAND FROM ABOVE)

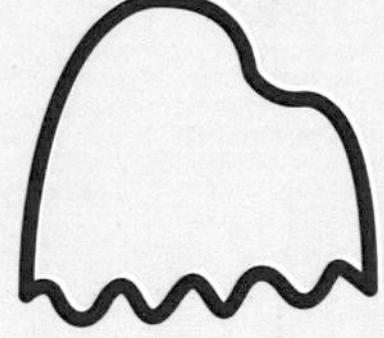

BREAKER OF LUCK

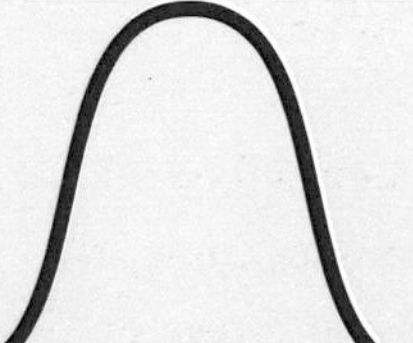

MILITARY

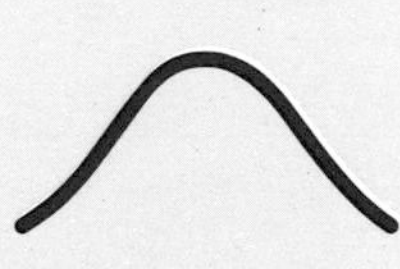

LEFT ASSISTANT

RIGHT ASSISTANT

The second ring contain the symbols of the nine stars that move through the cosmos affecting the fate of humans. When the stars are moving they are invisible, when they can be seen they are believed to be the seven stars of the Dipper plus two nearby stars. These nine stars also correspond to the nine different compass readings given in the Pa Che system described in chapter 3. Not only does each star wield a different influence, but its presence is also apparent in the shape of the land. The Dipper stars are:

THE SECOND RING

T'AN LUNG	COVETOUS WOLF
CHU-MEN	CHIEF GATE
LU-TS'UN	SALARY (RANK) PRESERVED
LIEN-CHEN	PURITY AND TRUTH
P'O-CHUN	BREAKER OF ARMIES OR FORTUNE
WEN-CH'U	CULTURAL ACTIVITIES
WU-CH'U	MILITARY ACTIVITIES
THE REMAINING STARS ARE:	
TSO-FU	LEFT ASSISTANT
YU'PI	RIGHT ASSISTANT

Their manifestation in the land is loosely covered by the forms shown on p.97. The third ring follows the position of the 24 mountains. These correspond to 4 hexagrams from the Later Heaven sequence, 8 heavenly stems and 12 earthly branches. The heavenly stems Wu and Ch'i are not represented here since they correspond to earth at the centre. As well as having a symbolic meaning, the mountains are also directional points similar to the directional points on the sundial or mariner's compass. The 24 points may also be grouped into threes so that a group of 8 corresponds to the 4 cardinal points and to what the Chinese call the 4 'corners' of the Earth. In more detailed compasses these 24 points may appear in three rings, always in the same order but shifted round several degrees. The three rings correlate to Heaven, Earth and Humans, all are equally effective and must act in harmony with one another to maintain the balance of the universe.

The Third Ring

BRANCHES	TRIGRAMS	STEMS	DIRECTION
		JEN	NNW BY N
TZU			N
		KUEI	NNE BY N
CH'OU			NNE BY E
	KEN		NE
YIN			ENE BY N
		CHIA	ENE BY E
MAO			E
		YI	ESE BY E
CH'EN			ESE BY S
	SUN		SE
SZU			SSE BY E
		PING	SSE BY S
WU			S
		TING	SSW BY S
WEI			SSW BY W
	K'UN		SW
SHEN			WSW BY S
		KENG	WSW BY W
YU			W
		HSIN	WNW BY W
HSU			WNW BY N
	CH'IEN		NW
HAI			NNW BY W

When readings are taken from the three ring, each symbol's influence is slightly blurred and it allows for a greater interaction with neighbouring symbols. Although this indicates a continual state of flux within the symbols, the cardinal points are considered to be unchanging and the 'corner' points changing. The symbols are arranged as shown in the table on p.99.

The fourth ring lists the eight major Tzu Wei stars from the Tzu Wei astrology system. Tzu Wei is the name of the god in charge of what is variously called the Purple Planet, the Purple Star or the Pole Star. The Pole Star is the centre of the astronomical system and the astrological calendar. Ursa Major and Ursa Minor, the two closest constellations are seen as the North and South Measures, which represent a human lifespan. The god of birth dwells in the Southern Measure and the god of death in the Northern Measure. The Pole Star is the centre of life and the stars that surround it are measured in relation to this central star. Each of the eight stars in this ring appears four times, which gives the geomancer the opportunity to choose alternative positions if one aspect gives an inauspicious reading.

The fifth and sixth rings each contain the 64 hexagrams (the 64 possible combinations that arise from combining the eight trigrams). Since all things are subject to change, except the Tao, the hexagrams listed in the fifth ring provide a reading for the present, the sixth ring provides a reading for what may happen in the future.

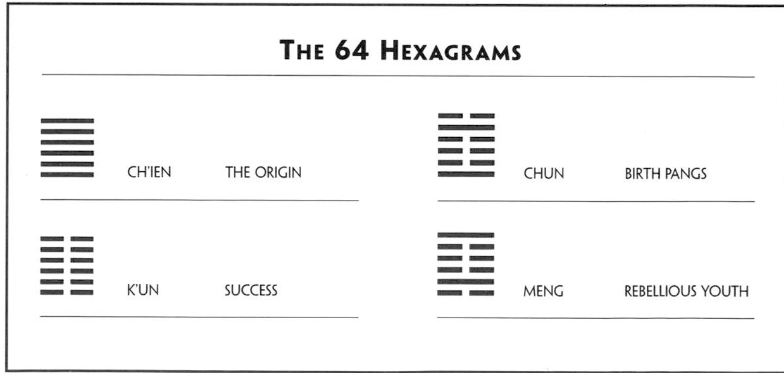

THE 64 HEXAGRAMS

CH'IEN	THE ORIGIN	CHUN	BIRTH PANGS
K'UN	SUCCESS	MENG	REBELLIOUS YOUTH

䷄	HSU	PATIENCE
䷅	SUNG	CONTENTION
䷆	SHIH	THE ARMY
䷇	PI	UNITY
䷈	HSIAO CH'U	HOLDING BACK THE LESS ABLE
䷉	LI	WALKING CAREFULLY
䷊	T'AI	BENEVOLENCE
䷋	P'I	OBSTRUCTION
䷌	T'UNG JEN	COMPANIONS
䷍	TA YU	MANY POSSESSIONS

䷎	CH'IEN	MODESTY
䷏	YU	ENTHUSIASM
䷐	SUI	ACCORDING OR AGREEING WITH
䷑	KU	DECAY
䷒	LIN	TO DRAW NEAR
䷓	KUAN	EXAMINE
䷔	SHIH HO	BITING THROUGH
䷕	PI	TO ADORN
䷖	PO	PEELING OR SPLITTING
䷗	FU	RETURN

WU WANG	NOT FALSE	CHIN	TO ADVANCE
TA CH'U	GREAT DOMESTICATING POWERS	MING I	BRIGHTNESS DIMMED
I	TAKING NOURISHMENT	CHAI JEN	THE FAMILY
TA KUO	GREAT EXPERIENCE	K'UEI	OPPOSITION
K'AN	WATERY DEPTHS	CHIEN	OBSTRUCTION
LI	TO SHINE BRIGHTLY, TO PART	HSIEH	LET LOOSE
HSIEN	ALL EMBRACING	SUN	INJURED
HENG	CONSTANT	I	INCREASE
TUN	TO HIDE	KUAI	NEW OUTCOME
TA CHUANG	GREAT STRENGTH	KOU	TO MEET

TS'UI	TO COLLECT
SHENG	RISING UP
K'UN	TO SURROUND AND WEAR OUT
CHING	THE WELL
KO	CHANGE
TING	THE COOKING POT
CHEN	SHOCK
KEN	RESTING
CHIEN	GRADUAL DEVELOPMENT
KUEI MEI	MARRYING THE YOUNGER SISTER
FENG	PROSPERITY
LU	THE TRAVELLER
SUN	GENTLE AND YIELDING
TUI	HAPPINESS
HUAN	SCATTERED
CHIEH	LIMITATIONS
CHUNG FU	INNER CONFIDENCE
HSAIO KOU	MINOR PROBLEMS
CHI CHI	ALREADY DONE
WEI CHI	NOT YET DONE

The Seventh Ring

CHIEH	LI CH'UN	BEGINNING OF SPRING
CH'I	YU SHUI	RAIN WATER
CH'I	CHING CHI	EXCITED INSECTS
CHIEH	CH'UN FEN	SPRING EQUINOX
CH'I	CH'ING MING	CLEAR AND BRIGHT
CH'I	KU YU	GRAIN RAINS
CHIEH	LI HSIA	SUMMER BEGINS
CH'I	HSAIO MAN	GRAIN FILLING
CH'I	MANG CHUNG	GRAIN IN EAR
CHIEH	HSAI CHI	SUMMER SOLSTICE
CH'I	HSIAO SHU	SLIGHT HEAT
CH'I	TA SHU	GREAT HEAT
CHIEH	LI CH'IU	AUTUMN BEGINS
CH'I	CH'U SHU	LIMIT OF HEAT
CH'I	PAI LU	WHITE DEW
CHIEH	CH'IU FEN	AUTUMN EQUINOX
CH'I	HAN LU	COLD DEW
CH'I	SHUANG CHIANG	HOAR FROST DESCENDS
CHIEH	LI TUNG	WINTER BEGINS
CH'I	HSAIO HSUEH	SLIGHT SNOW
CH'I	TA HSUEH	GREAT SNOW
CHIEH	TUNG CHIH	WINTER SOLSTICE
CH'I	HSIAO HAN	SLIGHT COLD
CH'I	TA HAN	GREAT COLD

The seventh ring contains the 24 terms of the solar calendar. These 24 phases were and still are used by farmers to guide them through the agricultural year. Each of the 24 terms corresponds to 15 degrees of the sun's motion in longitude on the ecliptic and in the calendar they occur every 15 or 16 days. Although this solar calendar is correlated with the other rings on the compass, it does not have the symbolic value of the other rings and is used purely for practical reasons. This cycle indicates to the geomancer the periods of growth and decay and is divided into 8 chieh and 16 ch'i. Ch'i indicates the periods of growth and decay, which in a greater sense is part of what yin and yang represent. Chieh marks the end of certain periods and heralds the beginning of new phases in the annual cycle.

The eighth ring contains the 28 constellations that are used for determining the position and time of the burial. The constellations are usually gathered into groups of seven to represent the four quarters of the compass. The constellations, or hsui, were asterims distributed around the celestial equator in 2400 BCE although their positions have changed so that they can no longer be regarded, if they originally were, as points marking the equator. The constellations are all visible throughout the year so each is considered to govern 28 differently sized portions of a circle with Heaven at the centre.

Constellations can bestow good luck or misfortune on a certain day, so if the first reading is unsuitable the geomancer can refer to the yearly Chinese Almanac to check the annual movement of the constellation in question and determine an alternative date that offers a positive reading.

The ninth ring divides up the 360 degrees of the circle. (The Chinese circle used to be divided into 365¼ degrees until the introduction of advanced astrological techniques by the Jesuits in China during the 16th and 17th centuries.)

THE 36-RINGED COMPASS

There are no set rules for the number of rings on a compass or their content, although it is unusual to find a compass with more than 38 rings. The compass illustrated on p.106 has 36 rings and their names and purposes are described in the list that follows:

THE LO PAN COMPASS

羅經透解全圖

第一層 先天八卦
第二層 洛書即後天卦
第三層 八煞黃泉
第四層 四路八路黃泉
第五層 九星分龍貴賤
第六層 地盤正針
第七層 陰陽龍
第八層 二十四山正五龍
第九層 刼煞盤
第十層 穿山七十二龍
第十一層 穿山周易卦
第十二層 中針人盤
第十三層 透地六十龍連偏正盤
第十四層 透地奇門
第十五層 透地連山卦
第十六層 透地龍配二十八宿
第十七層 貴人祿馬子父財官此盤字
多羅經不便刊錄請見書字

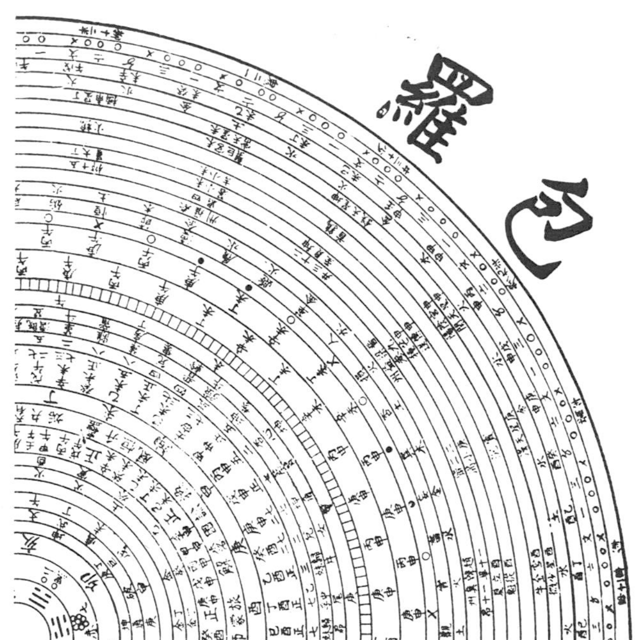

ABOVE THE 36-RINGED COMPASS IS AN ELABORATE DEVICE WITH MANY SYMBOLS.

1 Fu His hexagrams – (former hexagrams).

2 Wen Wang hexagrams – (later hexagrams).

3 The eight positions of the Baleful Spirits – help identify unlucky positions on the ground.

4 The four and eight ways of Wang Ch'uen – these are used to help find the deceased an auspicious position in the land of the dead so as to ensure a good rebirth.

5 The nine Star and Separating the Dragon Ring – these are used to identify whether the dragon is lucky or malign on the land or rivers surrounding the grave.

6 The Earth Valley Needle – this is the opposite of the Heaven Pool. This ring is used in the cemetery to find the most suitable position for the tombstone.

7 Yin and Yang Dragon Ring – this contains the heavenly stems and earthly branches.

8 The 24 Mountains and the five Dragons (elements) – the geomancer uses this ring to identify the elements that may attack or help the deceased.

9 The Baleful and Evil Ring – this ring identifies the spirits in the land that may cause misfortune or accidents within the family of the deceased.

10 The 72 points of the Dragon through the Mountain – the geomancer takes a reading from a hill to check the dragon ch'i coming from the hill in relation to the site.

11 Through the Mountain Later hexagrams – this is used to develop the reading taken from ring 10. This reading is also taken from a hill to determine auspicious points on the site within the range of the hexagram.

12 The Human Pool – this is used at the site to assess the horoscope of the living and occasionally the dead to determine if it is compatible with the eight character horoscope of the person concerned. Readings are taken of the hexagrams, stems and branches. If feng shui diagnosis is taken at the grave the geomancer is able to comment on how the position of the deceased can affect the fortune of the family.

13 The Earth Spirit of the 60 Dragons – this is used to discover the points where the earth spirits help or attack so that the coffin can be placed in a good position.

14 Through the Earth Door – this finds the right path for the dead to travel through the earth to the land of the spirits, Wang Ch'uen.

15 Through the Earth and Mountain hexagrams – these are used to asses which hexagrams are compatible with the Dragon points in the earth and in the mountain.

16 Through the Earth Dragon – this ring is combined with the 28 constellations. Using the position of the dragon and the 28 constellations, the geomancer can identify good or bad positions for the burial.

17 The Astrology ring – is used to check the balance of the elements, yin and yang, stems, branches and hexagrams so that a full horoscope reading can be taken at the site and in relation to the person concerned.

18 The Heaven Pool Adjusting Needle – this ring takes into account all the readings taken so far. This ring is usually marked with different coloured sections to denote yin and yang divisions on the compass.

19 The 246 degrees of the compass ring – is used to take a reading at 246 degrees to the headstone so that the lay of the land and the courses of rivers can be read at that point.

20 The 28 degrees of the deceased – if the geomancer is unable to find a positive angle using ring 19, he then uses the degrees of this ring to find the best position for the tombstone in relation to the rivers and land forms.

21 The 37 Angles of the Deceased – are used to calculate a suitable position for the tombstone taking into account footpaths, rivers, roads, spirits and the circulation of ch'i.

22 The Lonely and Prosperous Positions for the Dead – the 59 hexagrams that appear in this ring are correlated with the position of the burial site, the elements, the balance of yin and yang and the horoscope of the deceased.

23 The hexagrams appear again so that once the geomancer has found a suitable angle for the site he or she can check against the relevant hexagram to ensure it is in harmony with the deceased.

24 Heavenly Stems and Earthly Branches combine to find the five elements – since the elements change according to the combinations of stems and branches, this ring is used to check that the element associated with stem and branch relevant to the burial are compatible with the deceased.

25 The 12 Islands, also known as the 12 Palaces – used to identify which palace is associated with the deceased. (Each palace deals with a different aspect of a person. They are: the Ming palace, Brothers' and Sisters' palace, Marital palace, Man and Woman palace, Wealth palace, Sickness palace, Moving palace, Servants' palace, Officials' palace, Property palace, Fortune and Virtue palace, Parents' palace.)

26 The Life Star Ring – used to discover the life star or constellation of the deceased. The constellations in this ring do not direct or control the fate of the deceased.

27 The 24 Mountains – used to identify the angle at which the sun rises in relation to the grave.

28 The three Generals on Duty – the names of these three powerful spirits and guardians are repeated around the ring and one will be in charge of the deceased.

29 The 12 Gods in Command – these correlate with the 12 palaces of ring 25.

30 The Horse Palace Ring – the Horse is the travelling star that appears in 31 positions. The position of the star in relation to the grave will indicate whether the soul of the deceased will wander or be content and comfortable. This is important since the condition of the deceased will affect the fortunes of the living family.

31 The Heavenly Star with the Rolling Hexagrams – used to check your external environment and its influence upon your fortunes, this ring identifies which star is associated with each of eight hexagrams for your house.

32 The Heaven Degree Ring – this is used to discover the element that corresponds to the Heavenly Spirit that enters the point at which the reading is taken.

33 The 10 degrees of the 60 Dragon Points – once the geomancer has identified a suitable angle, he will automatically read the 10 degrees that span that position. The 10 degrees then correlate with one of the 60 dragon points.

34 This ring indicates the latitude and longitude of the site.

35 When the 10 Heavenly Stems and the 12 Earthly Branches are combined there are always two branches left over, and this ring lists the dead branches at various positions. The geomancer is able to check that the dead branches associated with the direction of the site do not appear in the eight character horoscope of the person concerned.

36 The 28 constellations that appear in this ring do not direct or control the deceased. They are used by the geomancer to correlate a constellation with the burial site of the deceased.

The Geomancer's Ruler

The exact proportions of a building, room or the height of furniture should be checked by the geomancer to ensure fortune and prosperity. To do this he uses a geomancer's ruler. This instrument not only marks distances but also implies lucky or unlucky measurements.

The Chinese character above the centimetres are for internal use, those marked under the inches are for external use (*see* illustration on p.113). The characters that are written in the boxes indicate whether this is a lucky or unlucky measurement. At the end of the fourth box of characters on the internal and external markings, the category of

Readings from the Lower Line Used for the Internal Measurements:

1–4	HARM
5–8	PROSPERITY
9–12	DISTRESS
13–16	REASON
17–20	OFFICIAL TITLE
21–24	DEATH
25–28	EXPANSION
29–32	LOSS
33–36	WEALTH
37–40	CHILDREN

Readings from the Upper Line Used for the External Measurements:

1–4	WEALTH
5–8	DISEASE
9–12	LEAVING
13–16	REASON
17–20	TITLE
21–24	ROBBERY
25–28	HARM
29–32	CAPITAL

fortune changes; for example the first four boxes marked on the external line in the diagram opposite represent different aspects of wealth and the four boxes that follow it represent different aspects of loss and disease. There is a character written in the middle of each

Geomancer's Ruler

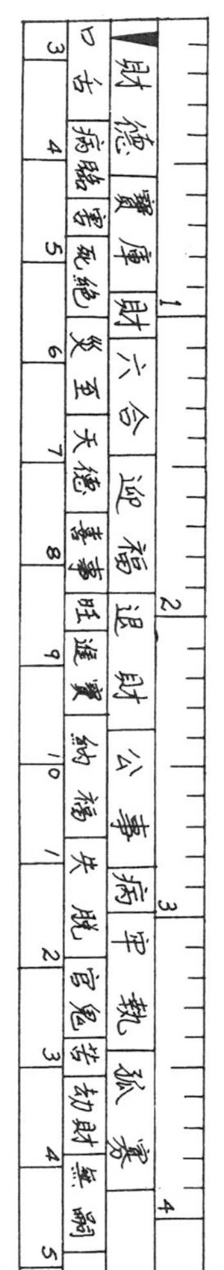

ABOVE THIS RULER DETAILS LUCKY AND UNLUCKY MEASUREMENTS.

group of four that denotes the overall fortune for that group. At the end of 32 boxes of characters on the external line and 40 boxes of characters on the internal line, the characters are repeated once again.

The Lo Shu Magic Square and Numbers

Other numerical calculations used by the geomancer in his assessment are based on the Lo Shu magical square.

The even, female or yin numbers are placed at the corner of the square and the odd, male or yang numbers are at the four cardinal points and the centre.

ABOVE WHEN ADDED TOGETHER IN A VERTICAL, HORIZONTAL OR DIAGONAL LINE, THE NUMBERS OF THE LO SHU MAGICAL SQUARE ALWAYS ADD UP TO 15.

The Legend of the Lo Shu Magical Square

Legend tells how the square was revealed some 4,000 years ago to Ta Yu, who became emperor of China.

Ta Yu, was working as an engineer on a project to build a tunnel through Dragon Gate Mountain, a project designed to tame the turbulent River Lo.

One day, Ta Yu found an entrance to a cave that wasn't marked on any of his plans. He entered the huge cave, and, guided by shafts of light that fell through narrow slits in the stone, he came to a narrow path at the back of the cavern. He noticed strange lines and diagrams carved in the damp walls of the passage and unexpectedly his light fell across the sleeping form of an animal. At first he thought it was a pig, but its skin had a faint yellow tinge and it held a bright, perfectly rounded pearl in its mouth.

Ta Yu stepped across the animal's body and continued until he caught sight of a fierce dog, crouching low as though ready to pounce. He stood perfectly still but the dog only barked as though trying to speak to him. The dog rose to its feet, span on its heels and loped on deeper into the mountain. Ta Yu then heard a movement from behind and turned to see the yellow pig standing close behind him. He had no choice but to follow the dog.

He walked along with them for countless miles and, although he had had nothing to eat or drink for a long time, he felt exhilarated. It was only when he caught sight of a bright white light ahead of him that his limbs suddenly felt heavy and his body exhausted.

Without warning, the dog stopped, turned to face Ta Yu and fixed him with piercing, green eyes. Ta Yu was transfixed and unable to see the pig who had slowly begun to take the shape of a man in flowing, black robes. Then, as he watched, the dog's fore and hind legs began to assume the shape of human limbs and gradually he, too, became a man in black robes. It was then that Ta Yu knew that his guards were the Jade Emperor's servants. A figure appeared ahead in a bright circle of light and Ta Yu was drawn to him. The creature had the face of a snake but the body of a man. Ta Yu knew he was in the presence of a deity. The deity lifted a parchment scroll from the floor beside him and beckoned Ta Yu to come closer. Eight groups of lines had been drawn in black ink on the scroll, some were straight and others broken. The creature had revealed the eight trigrams to Ta Yu.

'Are you the sage, the son of Wah Su?' asked Ta Yu.

'I am,' he replied, 'my mother was born and lived in a perfect land. One day a rainbow appeared and she stood in its light for two hours. The Jade Emperor sent a baby down the rainbow and after 12 years she gave birth to me.'

Ta Yu thought back to the legends he had learned as a child and realized he was in the presence of a great Emperor, famed for his wise rule throughout China. The Emperor then offered Ta Yu a jade tablet 12 units in length. Each unit represented the 12 divisions of the day and of the year. He then handed him a turtle shell inscribed with the Lo Shu magic square. Finally the emperor spoke,

'You have shown great wisdom and skill in taming the River Lo. The tunnel through the Dragon Gate mountain was your final test; you have proved yourself worthy of ruling China. The hexagrams on the scroll will help you to predict the auspicious years for your people, the jade tablet gives you the authority to govern wisely, the inscriptions on the turtle shell give you the ability to plan well.'

Cradling the precious gifts in his arms, Ta Yu left the emperor and returned to the outside world. As the emperor had predicted, Ta Yu was praised throughout China for his engineering feats and was soon declared Emperor. According to legend, the Emperor Yu reigned for 40 years and during his wise rule the land was never plagued by drought, flood or famine.

Nine and one are considered the most auspicious numbers since nine represents wholeness, something that is complete, and one is the beginning of all things.

If the numbers are added up in any line they come to 15. The square is based on an earlier design that incorporated a central fifth square. The simple square with a central fifth square probably developed into the square with

ABOVE THE LO SHU SQUARE WAS REVEALED TO EMPEROR TA YU INSCRIBED ON THE BACK OF A TURTLE'S SHELL.

THE LO SHU MAGIC SQUARE AND THE SEASONS

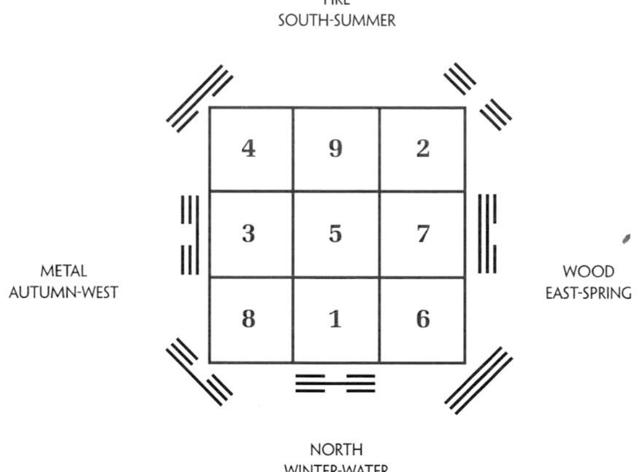

The Lo Shu magical square is also a diagrammatic representation of the seasons. The numbers, followed in clockwise direction, show the ratio of yang to yin in the annual cycle. In winter, yang is at its lowest (1) and yin at its highest (8); in the summer, yang is at its highest (9) and yin its lowest (2). The square also orders the trigrams of the Later Heaven sequence and the elements according to the compass directions.

nine divisions on the basis of a hand count. The little finger down to the thumb are the odd numbers 1, 3, 5, 7 and 9 and the hollows between the fingers and the thumb are the even numbers 2, 4, 6 and 8. The number 5 at the centre is the most powerful – it is translated as 'wu' in Chinese and the Chinese characters for 'midday' and for 'myself' are also read as 'wu'.

ABOVE BUILDINGS SHOULD IDEALLY BE DIVISIBLE INTO NINE EQUAL SECTORS, AS IN THE LO SHU MAGICAL SQUARE.

Aware of the power inherent in the Lo Shu magic square, architects and geomancers advised their rulers to build cities, temples, palaces and mansions according to this plan. For example, the Imperial Palace in Beijing is based on this square. In feudal times, a landowner who could afford nine rooms followed this layout, moving from room to room according to the seasons so that his rule over his subjects was wisely regulated.

Even though planning according to the Lo Shu square does not exert such a powerful influence in modern day design, the association with lucky and unlucky numbers is still effective in Chinese life. Numbers themselves or homonyms (words that have similar pronunciation) have an important bearing on personal or business decisions.

If the numbers in the time or date of a wedding or signing a contract add up to nine this is considered lucky. In contrast, numbers adding up to four or ending in four are considered unlucky since the Cantonese word for 'four' sounds like the word for 'die'.

FAMILY FESTIVALS

CHAPTER NINE

This chapter concerns the annual festivals that commemorate the dead. The relationship between the living and the dead is an important and effective part of Chinese family life. The needs of the ancestors are maintained by their relatives and in return for this continued care the spirit of the ancestors bestow good fortune on the living. By choosing a positive burial site, the feng shui expert ensures that the deceased not only rests peacefully but is provided with an appropriate gateway to the next world.

CHING MING

The festival of Ching Ming falls in the spring usually on the 5th or 6th April during the end of the second, or beginning of the third months of the lunar calendar. Ching Ming means 'clear and bright' and is one of the 24 phases of the year referred to on p.104. It is a time associated with the resurgence of life in spring and it is traditional for women and children to wear willow catkin. This is believed to give protection from being reborn as dogs at a future time.

ABOVE THE CHINESE TRADITIONALLY LIGHT RED CANDLES AND INCENSE STICKS AT THE GRAVES OF DECEASED ANCESTORS DURING THE ANNUAL CHING MING FESTIVAL.

The focus of the festival is a visit to the ancestral spirits who hover around the tombs. Cemeteries are often built close to farming land and since this is the beginning of the agricultural year the spirits of the dead can be called upon to help bring about a fruitful harvest.

When families visit the grave, they first sweep away the debris that has gathered on and around the grave during the previous year and repaint the inscriptions to the dead. Incense sticks and red candles are lit in front of the the headstone, which bears a photo of the deceased. Paper clothes and 'spirit' money are also burnt to provide the dead with fresh supplies for the afterlife. Rice, wine, tea, chicken, fruit and other food are also left on the grave. Many of these foods are chosen for their special associations with good fortune. One of the specialities at Ching Ming is bean curd with fish heads and tails. Fish implies profit and the heads and tails give the offering a sense of wholeness. The word 'fu' from 'tao fu', meaning 'wish' is that the ancestors, who are hopefully satisfied with the siting of their graves and comforted by their relatives, will protect their descendants.

After the offerings have been made a celebratory picnic is held on the hillside close to the grave so the spirits of the dead are present. Before the family leave, they tuck several strips of offering paper under a stone on top of the grave as a sign that the grave has been tended for that year.

This is also the day to visit the ancestral hall, if the family still have one. The ancestral hall is a building that contains tablets listing the names of the clan's founding ancestor and other deceased members of the family.

The founding ancestor's tablet is put in a position of prominence on the main altar and those who were distinguished in life, produced large families or were wealthy, also have positions of prominence on smaller altars to the left and right. The tablets belonging to the most prestigious members of the family are not removed from the main altar but the tablets of those who were not so highly regarded are shifted to the back of the hall to make room for tablets belonging to the recently deceased.

The well-being of the dead, the living and those yet to be born is linked through the existence of these ancestral halls. In as much as the family revolved around the founder of their clan during his life time, so it is after his death. These ancestral halls are not only places of remembrance, in the past they have been places of worship, community centres and council chambers, although with the widespread Chinese diaspora many Chinese are now unable to visit these halls.

The rituals that are performed here are performed on behalf of the whole clan. The dead souls maintain their vitality through the offering and ritual and the living will be guided and protected by their ancestors. Moreover, those who have yet to be born will have the blessings of their deceased relatives when their names are inscribed in the register of births kept in the ancestral hall.

Many families will also have a smaller ancestral shrine in their home and similar offerings are made and prayers said before these shrines at the time of Ching Ming.

THE HUNGRY GHOST FESTIVAL

The 15th day of the 7th lunar month is the time to remember the spirits of those who have left this world without a proper burial, or who have no relative to care for them. Ancestors who have relatives are considered 'tso sin' – former holy fathers – but those who are abandoned are 'kwai' – disembodied spirits or ghosts. Unlike the ancestors, they are not sustained by paper food and money or by offerings at the shrine. The living do not turn to them for help or advice and they have no place to rest. This lack of respect makes them bitter and they retaliate by creating danger in the world of the living, which is why they have to be placated.

The Seventh Moon is a particularly disturbing time for many Chinese since the gates of the underworld are opened to allow these unfortunates to wander in the world of the living. Their anger can be soothed if they are presented with the same offerings that are given to the ancestors and gods. Their anger is further assuaged if they are provided with several days of opera to entertain them.

In Hong Kong the celebrations are arranged by the elders of the area or by the Residents Association. House to house collections are made to subsidize this event and the amount received decides the scale of the celebrations. The celebrations take place in temporary constructions built around open spaces. A theatre is built at one end and an altar, where huge sticks of incense are constantly burnt, is constructed at the other end. Deities are carried in sedan chairs from local temples and reside in a temporary temple behind the altar. The organizing committee usually makes its office at one side of the shrine and the remaining space is occupied by piles of offerings, Buddhist and Taoist headquarters and a huge paper statue of Tai Si Wong. It is believed that Tai Si Wong, who holds a notebook and pen, records the deeds of those at the festival. There is usually a statue of the bodhisattva, Kuan Yin, the goddess of mercy, close by. Some say that she once held a feast for the Hungry Ghosts but they behaved so badly that she was forced to invite the King of Hell to her next party to maintain order. From that time on the ghosts have behaved correctly in her company. Others say that although Kuan Yin is a compassionate deity, there are times when she has to appear fierce to correct unruly behaviour and so she appears at the Hungry Ghost festival as Tai Si Wong.

In the lead up to the festival, in the first two weeks of the seventh moon, families make private offerings to the ghosts in a ceremony known as shiu yi, 'burning clothes'. Those who live close to the sea sail out to pray and scatter rice on the waters or launch small paper boats carrying food and paper offerings to appease the ghosts who have been lost at sea.

On the last evening of this festival, usually on the 15th day of the 7th moon, the paper 'Bank of Hell' notes, paper clothes, furniture, transport and food are sent to the ghosts. The paper goods are burnt. Once the food has been offered, and the ghosts spiritually satisfied, it is shared amongst those present. As the festival draws to its close a huge paper statue of Tai Si Wong is carried from one end of the bonfire to the other so he can assess the efforts that have been made. Then he, too, is burnt so he can make his report to Heaven.

CH'UNG YEUNG – THE DOUBLE NINTH

During the first nine days of the ninth month the gods lift restrictions on those who abide in the underworld and the living are able to communicate with their dead relatives.

On the ninth day, many Chinese visit the graves of their ancestors and clear away the decaying growth of the summer. Bank of Hell notes are burnt and paper clothes are offered to protect the dead against the oncoming cold of winter. Once the family have paid their respects they share a picnic at the grave. This is the second remembrance festival of the year, and it varies from family to family whether one or both of these days is celebrated.

This is also the time for families who live near enough their ancestral hall to visit and to make offerings to their clan ancestor and others whose names are listed there.

ADDRESSES

AUSTRALASIA

Feng Shui Design Studio
PO Box 705
Glebe
Sydney NSW 2037
Australia
Tel: 61 2 315 8258

Feng Shui Society of Australia
PO Box 1565
Rozelle
Sydney NSW 2039
Australia

UK

The Geomancer
PO Box 250
Woking
GU21 1YJ
Tel: 44 1483 839898
Fax: 44 1483 488998

Feng Shui Association
31 Woburn Place
Brighton
BN1 9GA
Tel/Fax: 44 1273 693844

Feng Shui Network International
PO Box 2133
London
W1A 1RL
Tel: 44 171 935 8935
Fax: 44 171 935 9295

Feng Shui Society
18 Alacross Road
London
W5 4HT
Tel/Fax: 44 181 567 2034

Midlands Feng Shui
34 Banbury Road
Ettington
Stratford-upon-Avon
Warwickshire
CV37 7SU
Tel/Fax: 44 1789 740116

NORTH AMERICA

Earth Design
PO Box 530725
Miami Shores
FL 33153
Tel: 1 305 756 6426
Fax: 1 305 751 9995

Feng Shui Designs
PO Box 399
Nevada City
CA 95959
Tel: 1 800 551 2482

The Feng Shui Institute of America
PO Box 488
Wabasso
FL 32970
Tel: 1 407 589 9900
Fax: 1 407 589 1611

Feng Shui Warehouse
PO Box 3005
San Diego
CA 92163
Tel: 1 800 399 1599
Fax: 1 800 997 9831

Macrobiotic Association of Connecticut
24 Village Green Drive
Litchfield
CT 06759
Tel: 1 860 567 8801

Transformational Institute
20 Butlertown Road
Waterford
CT 06385
Tel: 1 203 44 37330

Vital Environments Inc
PO Box 277
Stanhope
NJ 07874

Bibliography

Baker, Hugh, *More Ancestral Images*, South China Morning Post Publications, 1980, and *Ancestral Images Again*, South China Morning Post Limited, Hong Kong, 1981

Bary, Theodore de (ed.), *Sources of Chinese Tradition*, Columbia University Press, 1960

Burkhardt, V.R., *Chinese Creeds and Customs*, South China Morning Post Publications, Hong Kong, 1982

Chamberlain, Jonathon, *Chinese Gods*, Long Island Publishers, Hong Kong, 1983

Dore, Henry S.J., *Chinese Customs*, (trans.) by M.Kennelly, S.J., Graham Brash Publishers, Singapore, 1987

Eberhard, J., *Chinese Fairy Tales and Folk Tales*, London, 1937

Feuchtwang, Stephen D.R., *An Anthropological Analysis of Chinese Geomancy*, Southern Materials Center, Inc., Taipei, 1st edition, 1974

Henry, B.C., *The Cross and the Dragon*, New York, 1885

Law, Joan, and Ward, Barbara E., *Chinese Festivals*, South China Morning Post Publications, Hong Kong, 1982

Legge, James, *The Chinese Classics*, Oxford University Press, 1871, Southern Materials Center, Inc., Taipei, 1983, Vols. III and V

Lip, Evelyn, *Chinese Geomancy*, Times Books International, 1979

Man-Ho, Kwok, *Authentic Chinese Horoscopes*, Arrow, London, 1987

Needham, Joseph, *Science and Civilisation in China*, Cambridge University Press, 1956, Vol. II, 1959, Vol.III

O'Brien, Joanne, *Chinese Myths and Legends*, Arrow, London, 1990

Palmer, Martin, Kwok Man-Ho, O'Brien, Joanne, *The Fortune Teller's I Ching*, Century, London, 1986

INDEX